WORDS
FOR
WAR

Ukrainian Research Institute
Harvard University

 Borderlines Foundation for
Academic Studies

 National Endowment for
the Humanities

Ukrainian Studies

Series Editor
Vitaly Chernetsky (University of Kansas)

WORDS
FOR
WAR
New Poems
from Ukraine

Edited by
Oksana Maksymchuk and
Max Rosochinsky

Boston - 2018

Library of Congress Cataloging-in-Publication Data

Classification: LCC PG3934.4.W37 (ebook) | LCC PG3934.4.W37 W67 2017 (print) | DDC 891.7/91080358--dc23
LC record available at https://lccn.loc.gov/2017041923

Published by the Ukrainian Research Institute, Harvard University with the Borderlines Foundation for Academic Studies and Academic Studies Press

The publication of this book has been made possible in part by a major grant from the Scholarly Editions and Translation program of the National Endowment for the Humanities: Celebrating 50 Years of Excellence.

Any views, findings, conclusions, o r r ecommendations e xpressed i n this book do not necessarily represent those of the National Endowment for the Humanities or of the Ukrainian Research Institute, Harvard University.

ISBN 9781618116673 (E-book)
ISBN 9781618116680 (Open Access)
ISBN 9781618118615 (paper)

Book design and illustrations by Grycja

Layout by Kryon Publishing Services (P) Ltd.
www.kryonpublishing.com

CONTENTS

PREFACE

Most of us in the Western world have little firsthand knowledge of war. Normally, we are not forced to face war, fight in a war, flee from war. *We* don't get tortured, see our homes and schools collapse, lose relatives and friends to war, spend months locked up in basements "because this is war." When we do get involved, as soldiers, journalists, or relief workers, we *go* to war or *get sent* to war – war does not come to us. Those of us who do not *go* and have not been to war are nevertheless aware of war, sometimes at a deep level. Yet this awareness is usually indirect: it requires inference. Like with a disease, we first encounter symptoms, these heralds of disruption reaching us from regions both intimate and strange. Even as we trace the tremors and the fevers back to the original cause, the source of the disturbance itself stays hidden from view. Many of us in the West have lived with wars for significant parts of our lives, wars that mostly remained out of sight. These hidden wars have become a part of us, shaping our minds, affecting the words, images, and concepts with which we think. The ways in which we create meaning have undergone shifts and mutations in an attempt to represent this new reality, outer as well as inner. Yet our words and sentences do not just describe or explain what there is. They are also traces of what is absent, what stays distant or remains hidden. *Words for War*, then, is not only an interpretative response to war—it is also one of the many effects of the war that had been endured. Like broken furniture and mutilated bodies, these poems are traces of what had happened, as well as evidence that it did really happen. They are a form of testimony, even if what they testify about is not ordinarily witnessed historical events but rather cognitive transformations and semiotic shifts experienced by people in liminal situations.

People living in the midst of war are never abstract "people," just as the war is never an abstract "war" for them. Equally, the voices collected in this volume do not belong to some abstract "poets." These words come from specific people who dwell in a specific place. The place happens to be one that we, the editors, call home, even if we no longer go home to it: Ukraine, which on our inner map includes Crimea. It was there, in Yalta, that we first met and fell in love, and for the next two years our romance unfolded between two Ukrainian strongholds of monocultural identity, Simferopol in Crimea and Lviv in Western

Ukraine. Over the years, we have learned to navigate the precarious semiotic landscapes of these two worlds. While our American friends thought that as a Russian and a Ukrainian, we are basically cultural twins, to our relatives and friends back home, ours was a marriage of hostile traditions, and a reconciliation of opposing worldviews. The equilibrium was a fragile one, and the very tensions we saw playing out in the public discussions would occasionally unfold in our own family. We would find ourselves exchanging the conflicting slogans—about memory, history, language, violence, justice—in raised voices, surprised by the hold they have on us. When the annexation of Crimea in 2014 was followed by the large-scale eruption of military conflict in the east of Ukraine, engulfing whole cities, we knew it wasn't just a matter of one vicious leader's opportunism—it was also about the people who sought salvation, ignorant of the price they would pay for it. Alienated, resentful, and desperate to be saved from a world they had stopped recognizing as their own, they were ripe for manipulation; schooled in distrust and cynicism in their cramped Soviet kitchens, they nevertheless believed their Russian-tuned TV sets promising them a special destiny and an imperial future. For us, *Words for War* started out as a form of therapy. We sought to patch together the pieces of this disintegrating world, with its dangerously sharp yet blurred edges, and to amplify voices that rang true amid the din of fake news, hate speech, jejune Facebook affirmations, and blank-faced propaganda.

Poets are not a lofty apolitical tribe whose only concern is their literary craft. Far from remaining blind to the world of strife and conflict they inhabit, they are often the ones most radically affected—and thus changed—by it. As historically, politically, and socially situated individuals, they are also agents of change. Their acts matter, as do their words. We often find ourselves looking at the poets' lives to interpret poems, and at poems to understand their lives. Some of the poets whose work we have included in this anthology have been actively involved in the war in the east of Ukraine as volunteers, reading to the soldiers at the front, collecting and distributing humanitarian aid to the people affected by the war. Others have been less directly involved, but no less directly affected, since chaos has a tendency to spread, to change the perceived norms of life and creep into previously peaceful contexts. One poet—Borys Humenyuk—is a soldier himself. As we write this paragraph, we reflect on Borys' Facebook post from this morning: he hates meeting new people at the front, he said, because often when he calls them a few weeks later to say hello, no one picks up. War kills, and this changes experiences that are essential to us as social beings: of building connections, making friends. But war also causes other, more insidious types of harm to human relations. Many of the poets have lost relatives, finding themselves on different sides of the barricades; still more lost friends.

The war affects the whole population, but the way it affects poets warrants a special kind of attention. Through the practice of their art, poets are often uniquely sensitive to changes and shifts in how we, collectively, create meaning with words and images. In this, poets resemble well-crafted and finely tuned devices that register the relevant fluctuations with greater precision than the rest of us do. Because they work with language, it seems to happen almost automatically, involving little conscious reflection: the change in inputs simply leads to a change in outputs. As a result, even small changes register on their radars sooner, while great changes may lead to the destruction of the instrument of measurement altogether—just as looking directly at the sun can make an eye go blind. When confronted with excessive axiological shifts and intense borderline experiences, poets have sometimes found themselves unable to speak, and, in the most radical cases, unable to live.

To compare poets to measuring devices is not to deny them agency, or to repeat Heidegger's mystical insight that we do not speak language, but rather "language speaks us." Many poets are conscious of what it is they are striving to achieve: they have artistic goals and poetic projects, and they write for specific target audiences. However, poetry often requires something qualitatively different, an element of freedom. Poets describe the experience of writing as a kind of trance, involving letting go of oneself as an individual, giving up one's autonomy. Psychologists use the term "flow" to describe the intense absorption in one's work: experiments show that it involves an altered cognitive state, like falling in love or experiencing erotic arousal. There is a reason why the ancients— and more recently, the Romantics—talked of *inspiration*, of finding oneself inhabited by a being whose powers exceed one's own. It is never safe to assume identity between the "I" of the poem and the "I" of the poet. Poets often find that they don't just speak as themselves; sometimes they can't even recognize the voices they speak in. Because of their heightened sensitivity to the reverberations of meaning in its different modalities, poets absorb more than can reasonably serve as a basis for a single individual identity—and this may lead them to project voices that could be contradictory, even immoral in the eyes of some of their readers. Their creative process reflects this all-embracing sensitivity, to the point that it may seem to amount to moral unscrupulousness or resemble a multiple personality disorder.

Revealing the cost of war is a case in point. The poets in this anthology often take on this task deliberately and self-consciously, attempting to fill out the lacunae formed by the official bureaucratic discourse. Yet accomplishing the task takes them beyond their individual perspective, and outside the scope of their explicit consciously adopted goals. The bureaucratic account of the costs of war offers a sense of mastery over the unfathomable. As we try to understand the scope of the tragedy, we find it comforting to focus on quantitative measures: the numbers of the dead, the wounded, the displaced. Poets shift our attention to the domain of the Self that survives, and the cost of its survival. One mode of survival involves the reconstitution of identity in response to symbolic changes. Like a jellyfish that takes on a tint, once submerged in tinted water; like a neuron in a lab that takes on a dye to enable the scientists to trace its connections—so a poet absorbs the changes and displays them in the body of her works. In "Decomposition," Lyuba Yakimchuk presents herself as exhausted and bled dry, suddenly an old woman, with just one fragment of her previous youthful identity remaining ("No longer Lyuba / just a -ba"). In her cycle "I wake up . . . ," Marianna Kiyanovska's lyrical narrator emerges as a war-bound androgynous human being, feeding death from a palm, as one would a pet—except she has cut her palm open, exposing live flesh. And in the poem "I fly away . . . ," Vasyl Holoborodko, who fled the separatist-occupied Luhansk and is now de facto homeless, tries on different fairy-tale identities that would enable him to escape: now as a bird, and now as dandelion seed. These changes in the poets' descriptions of the beings standing behind their lyrical voice as aged, unsexed, and stripped of human form help expose war's effects on those who don't make it into our statistics. Poetry does not just mourn the dead—it exposes the losses of the survivors.

In the poems collected in this anthology, war is rarely the focal point. More often, war causes a sort of a semiotic ripple, transforming the page into something different than it appears at the first glance. More precisely, not just something different, but something additional to what the page offers initially, in the same way that the duck-rabbit is an image of *both* a duck and a rabbit. This ripple is not merely thematic, nor is it confined to semantics. There are shifts in prosody, in punctuation, syntactical breaks and cracks. In a Facebook post in 2016, Lyudmyla Khersonska noted how the war has plunged many Ukrainian poets into a state of innocence, a second childhood, in which they confront the need of learning to speak the language anew. Khersonska's own poems—now taking the perspective of a refugee girl trying to make a home for a "refugee" cat, now of a child that sees uncannily disfigured toy soldiers encircling her in her dream (to protect? to harm?)—epitomize this tendency. The need to remaster a language that had lost its previous vibrancy comes with the recognition that this language has acquired a new quality: now it's crisper, sharper, and with the potential to turn toxic. This emerging language needs to be handled carefully, responsibly; and expertise in this language is not to be taken for granted—it must be earned.

Poetry is defined not only by what it is but also by what it is not. In times of conflict, it is vital to resist easy answers—yet it's precisely such answers that we most crave in uncertain times. Ideologies seduce by generating surrogate or simpler meanings for terms we normally take to be multifaceted and complex: "good" and "bad," "normal" and "abnormal," "citizen" and "parasite." As society grows more polarized in response to the agenda pushed by ideologues, there is a growing psychological pressure to conform, to identify oneself as "one of us" and share the beliefs and values of the dominant group. Ethically problematic treatment of the supposedly undeserving "others" only increases one's commitment and sense of loyalty—in a similar way that shared experience of shame and guilt promotes intragroup bonding. Ideology manipulates *our* emotions and pushes *our* buttons—the personal pronouns it operates with are mostly plural. By contrast, an experience of reading poetry can open us up to another as an individual, letting us experience another's private world as our own. It lets us hear voices that the ideological loudspeaker had previously muffled or distorted. But ideologically motivated poems can also implicate us further, which attests to poetry's great power to shape desires and beliefs, to crystallize fears and anxieties. Since ancient times, epos was successful in consolidating political alliances and imperial allegiances; and odes promoted identification with particular leaders, and solidified personality cults. Poets, like most people, can be seduced by power, and must tread carefully in deciding what to throw their weight behind.

While poets do not always succeed in retaining their personal integrity in the face of ideological pressure, they may nevertheless remain great artists. Poetic language often reveals that our present situation is only one of many possibilities by helping us envision other ways to be, think, and feel. It reminds us that the world is not simply given to us—we are involved in making it what it is. In reflecting on the current experiences, poets often manage to create the language for future ones: the experience of surviving the war, of fixing up homes and rebuilding relationships, of healing and forgiving. It is in their words that we will find ourselves expressing grief and solidarity, anger and love.

In selecting the poems for this anthology, we have attempted to represent a variety of voices: young and old, female and male, somber and ironic, tragic and playful. We have tried to pay special attention to poems describing women's experiences of war: as mothers and daughters, soldiers and victims of war crimes, spouses and lovers, citizens and experts. The voices we assembled in this volume belong to some of the most prominent Ukrainian poets writing today. Yet our selection is by no means exhaustive. Many important and honored poets were left out. And over the two years that we have worked on the project, new and compelling voices emerged. Recognizing that the poetic response to the ongoing war is dynamic, we will keep introducing these new names in the online edition of this collection. We ask readers to refer to the anthology website for fresh translations, essays, and latest discoveries.

Oksana Maksymchuk
Max Rosochinsky

BAROMETERS

1.

My family huddled by the doorframe at 4 a.m., debating whether or not to open the door to the stranger wearing only his pajama pants, who'd been pounding on the door for at least five minutes, waking the whole apartment complex. Seeing the light come on, he began shouting through the door.

"Remember me? I helped you haul your refrigerator from Pridnestrovie. Remember? We talked about Pasternak on the drive. Two hours! Tonight they bombed the hospital. My sister is a nurse there. I stole someone's truck and drove across the border. I don't know anyone else. Can I make a phone call?"

So the war stepped its shoeless foot into my childhood two decades ago, under the guise of a half-naked man gulping on the phone, victim of an early post-Soviet "humanitarian aid" campaign.

2.

During a recent visit to Ukraine, my friend the poet Boris Khersonsky and I agreed to meet at a neighborhood café in the morning to talk about Pasternak (as if he is all anyone talks about, in our part of the world). But when I walked up the sidewalk at 9 a.m., the sidewalk tables were overturned and rubble was strewn into the street from where the building had been bombed.

A crowd, including local media, was gathered around Boris as he spoke out against the bombings, against yet another fake humanitarian aid campaign of Putin's. Some clapped; others shook their heads in disapproval. A few months later, the doors, floors, and windows of Boris's apartment were blown up.

There are many stories like this. They're often shared in short, hurried sentences, and then the subject is changed abruptly.

How can one speak about, write about, war? "Truthful war books," Orwell wrote, "are never acceptable to non-combatants."[1]

When Americans ask about recent events in Ukraine, I think of these lines from Boris's poem:

people carry explosives around the city
in plastic shopping bags and little suitcases.

3.

Over the last twenty years, Ukraine has been governed by both the Russian-speaking East and the Ukrainian-speaking West. The government periodically uses "the language issue" to incite conflict and violence, an effective distraction from the real problems at hand. The most recent conflict arose in response to the inadequate policies of President Yanukovych, who has since escaped to Russia. Yanukovych was universally acknowledged as the most corrupt president the country has ever known (he'd been charged with rape and assault, among other things, all the way back to Soviet times). However, these days, Ukraine's new government continues to include oligarchs and professional politicians with shrewd pedigrees and questionable motivations.

When the standoff between the Yanukovych government and crowds of protesters first began in 2013, and the embattled President left the country shortly thereafter, Putin sent his troops into Crimea, a Ukrainian territory, under the pretext of passionately protecting the Russian-speaking population. Soon, the territory was annexed. In a few months, under the pretext of humanitarian aid, more Russian military forces were sent into another Ukrainian territory, Donbas, where a proxy war has began.

All along the protection of Russian language was continually cited as the sole reason for the annexation and hostilities.

Does the Russian language in Ukraine need this protection? In response to Putin's occupation, many Russian-speaking Ukrainians chose to stand with their Ukrainian-speaking neighbors, rather than against them. When the conflict began to ramp up, I received this e-mail:

I, Boris Khersonsky, work at Odessa National University where I have directed the department of clinical psychology since 1996. All that time I have been teaching in Russian, and no one has ever reprimanded me for "ignoring" the official Ukrainian language of the state. I am more or less proficient in the Ukrainian language, but most of my students prefer lectures in Russian, and so I lecture in that language.

I am a Russian language poet; my books have been published mostly in Moscow and St. Petersburg. My scholarly work has been published there as well.

Never (do you hear me—NEVER!) did anyone go after me for being a Russian poet and for teaching in Russian language in Ukraine. Everywhere I read my poems in RUSSIAN and never did I encounter any complications.

However, tomorrow I will read my lectures in the state language— Ukrainian. This won't be merely a lecture — it will be a protest action in solidarity with the Ukrainian state. I call for my colleagues to join me in this action.

A Russian-language poet refuses to lecture in Russian as an act of solidarity with occupied Ukraine. As time passed, other such e-mails began to arrive from poets and friends. My cousin Peter wrote from Odessa:

Our souls are worried, and we are frightened, but the city is safe. Once in a while some idiots rise up and announce that they are for Russia. But we in Odessa never told anyone that we are against Russia. Let Russians do whatever they want in their Moscow and let them love our Odessa as much as they want—but not with this circus of soldiers and tanks!

Another friend, the Russian-speaking poet Anastasia Afanasieva, wrote from the Ukrainian city of Kharkiv about Putin's "humanitarian aid" campaign to protect her language:

In the past five years, I visited the Ukrainian-speaking Western Ukraine six times. I have never felt discriminated against because I spoke the Russian language. Those are myths. In all the cities of Western Ukraine I have visited, I spoke with everyone in Russian—in stores, in trains, in cafes. I have found new friends. Far from feeling aggression, everyone instead treated me with respect. I beg you, do not listen to the propaganda. Its purpose is to separate us. We are already very different, let's not become opposite, let's not create a war on the territory where we all live together. The military invasion which is taking place right now is the catastrophe for us all. Let's not lose our minds, let's not be afraid of non-existent threats, when there is a real threat: the Russian army's invasion.

As I read the letter after letter I couldn't stop thinking about Boris's refusal to speak his own language as an act of protest against the military invasion. What does it mean for a poet to refuse to speak his own language?

Is language a place you can leave? Is language a wall you can cross? What is on the other side of that wall?

4.

Every poet refuses the onslaught of language. This refusal manifests itself in silence illuminated by the meanings of poetic lexis—the meanings not of what the word says, but of what it withholds. As Maurice Blanchot wrote, "To write is to be absolutely distrustful of writing, while entrusting oneself to it entirely."[2]

Ukraine today is a place where statements like this one are put to the test. Another writer, John Berger, says this about the relationship of a person to one's language: "One can say of language that it is potentially the only human home." He insisted that it was "the only dwelling place that cannot be hostile to man . . . One can say anything to language. This is why it is a listener, closer to us than any silence or any god."[3] But what happens when a poet refuses his language as a form of protest?

Or, to put this question in broader terms: what happens to language in wartime? Abstractions very quickly attain physical attributes. This is how the Ukrainian poet Lyudmyla Khersonska sees her own body watching the war around her: *Buried in a human neck, a bullet looks like an eye, sewn in.* The poet Kateryna Kalytko's war is also a physical body: *War often comes along and lies down between you like a child/ afraid to be left alone.*

The language of poetry may or may not change us, but it shows the changes within us: the poet Anastasia Afanasieva writes using the first-person plural "we," showing us how the occupation of a country affects all its citizens, no matter which language they speak:

when a four-wheeler with a mortar
passed down the street
we didn't ask who are you
whose side are you on
we fell down on the floor and lay there.

5.

On another visit to Ukraine, I saw a former neighbor of mine, now crippled by war, holding his hand out on the street. He wasn't wearing any shoes. As I hurried by, hoping he wouldn't recognize me, I was suddenly brought up short by his empty hand. As if he were handing me his war.

As I walked away from him, I had an eerie feeling of recognition. How similar his voice, the voices of the Ukrainian poets I've been speaking with, to the voices of people in Afghanistan and Iraq, whose houses my own tax money has destroyed.

6.

In the late twentieth century, the Jewish poet Paul Celan became a patron saint of writing in the midst of crisis. Composing in the German language, he has broken speech to reflect the experience of a new, violated world. This effect is happening again—this time in Ukraine—before our very eyes.

Here is the case of poet Lyuba Yakimchuk, whose family are refugees from Pervomaisk, the city which is one of the main targets of Putin's most recent "humanitarian aid" effort. Answering my questions about her background, Lyuba responded:

I was born and raised in the war-torn Luhansk region and my hometown of Pervomaisk is now occupied. In May 2014 I witnessed the beginning of the war . . . In February 2015 my parents and grandmother, having survived dreadful warfare, set out to leave the occupied territory. They left under shelling fire, with a few bags of clothes. A friend of mine, a [Ukrainian] soldier, almost shot my grandma as they fled.

Discussing literature in wartime, Yakimchuk writes: "Literature rivals with the war, perhaps even loses to war in creativity, hence literature is changed by war." In her poems, one sees how warfare cleaves her words: "don't talk to me about Luhansk," she writes, "it's long since turned into *hansk/ Lu* had been razed to the ground / to the crimson pavement." The bombed-out city of Pervomaisk "has been split into *pervo* and *maisk*" and the shell of Debaltsevo is now her "*deb, alts, evo*." Through the prism of this fragmented language, the poet sees herself:

> I stare into the horizon
> . . . I have gotten so very old
> no longer Lyuba
> just a −*ba*.

Just as Russian-language poet Khersonsky refuses to speak his language when Russia occupies Ukraine, Yakimchuk, a Ukrainian-language poet, refuses to speak an unfragmented language as the country is fragmented in front of her eyes. As she changes the words, breaking them down and counterpointing the sounds from within the words, the sounds testify to a knowledge they do not possess. No longer lexical yet still legible to us, the wrecked word confronts the reader mutely, both within and beyond language.

Reading this poem of witness, one is reminded that poetry is not merely a description of an event; it is an event.

7.

What exactly is the poetry's witness? The language of poetry may or may not change us, but it shows the changes within us. Like a seismograph, it registers violent occurrences. Miłosz titled his seminal text *The Witness of Poetry* "not because we witness it, but because it witnesses us."[4] Living on the other side of the Iron Curtain, Zbigniew Herbert told us something similar: a poet is like a barometer for the psyche of a nation. It cannot change the weather. But it shows us what the weather is like.

8.

Can examining the case of a lyric poet really *show* us something that is shared by many—the psyche of a nation? the music of a time?

How is it that a lyric poet's spine trembles like a barometer's needle? Perhaps this is because lyric poet is a very private person: in her or his privacy this individual creates a language—evocative enough, strange enough—that enables her or him to speak, privately, to many people at the same time.

9.

Living many hundreds of miles from Ukraine, away from this war, in my comfortable American backyard, what right do I have to write about this war?— and yet I cannot stop writing about it: cannot stop mulling over the words by poets of my country in English, this language they do not speak. Why this obsession? Between sentences is the silence I do not control. Even though it is a different language, the silence between sentences is still the same: it is the space in which I see a family still huddled by the doorframe at 4 am, debating whether or not to open the door to the stranger, wearing only his pajama pants, who is shouting through the doorframe.

— Ilya Kaminsky

Notes

1 George Orwell, *As I Please: Essays, Journalism and Letters,* ed. Sonia Orwell and Ian Angus, vol. 3 (Boston: Nonpareil Books, 2000), 241.

2 Maurice Blanchot, *The Writing of the Disaster*, tr. Ann Stock (Lincoln: University of Nebraska Press, 1995), 110.

3 John Berger, *And Our Faces, My Heart, Brief as Photos* (New York: Vintage Books, 1991), 95.

4 Czesław Miłosz, *The Witness of Poetry: The Charles Eliot Norton Lectures,* 1981–82 (Cambridge, Mass.: Harvard University Press, 1983), 4.

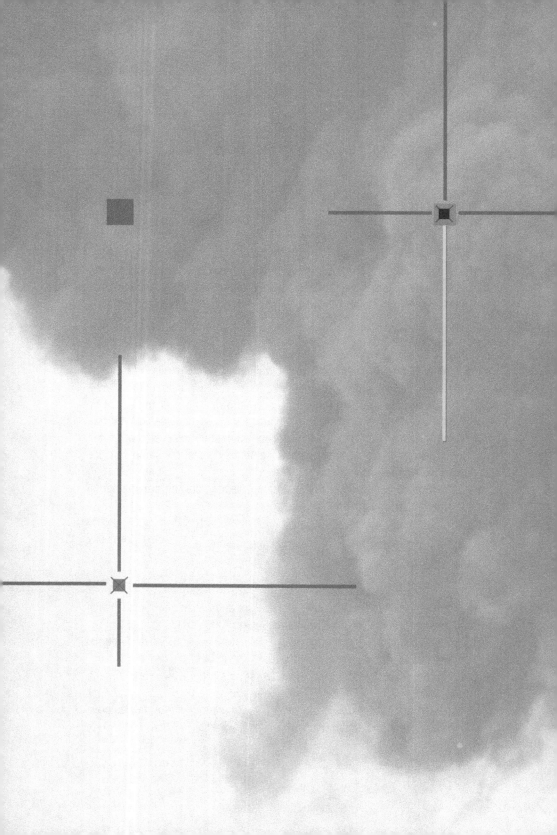

ANASTASIA
AFANASIEVA

* * *

she says
we don't have the right kind of basement in our building
I had to leave, no one can hide in there
we couldn't leave for a whole week straight
men elbowed us out
we were weaker, there was no room for us
in the past we thought about nice furniture
home improvements and such
now we think
our basement doesn't work
it won't protect us, it'll collapse on us
it's worse than sitting outside

we dragged our mattresses and pillows onto the floor
so that we could fall down as soon as it all starts
we fell down and lay there

my husband stayed behind
someone had to stay home
otherwise there'd be no home to come back to
there may be nowhere to go back to anyway
he watches the apartment
so no one moves in and takes our things
he calls once a week from some high-rise
where he magically gets cell reception
he says a few words and hangs up
I am alive
call back next Saturday

when a four-wheeler with a mortar
passed down the street

we didn't ask who are you
whose side are you on
we fell down to the floor and lay there

on our way to the market
the bullets whistled over our heads
we arrived here with a single bag
there wasn't enough room for people, let alone things

she speaks
as the August air
enters the room
in the yard
my coworkers are gathering overripe plums
last year those were perfect
this time around
we missed our harvest
now it's too late

I listen, and I don't know
if heaven and hell really exist
they must be separated by a journey
in a minivan, packed full of people
where plums ripen in silence
where people fall to the ground
and we're experiencing these moments
after death

Translated from the Russian by
Oksana Maksymchuk and Max Rosochinsky

* * *

Your inner void is larger
than the hole in your pocket,
larger than a black hole —
you hang laundry in the yard
as in your heyday in the thirties
when the Earth burned under your feet.

You no longer remain,
nor breathe, nor look back.
You proceed without cease
onward toward bright victory —
the color of sickly blue flesh,
blood spilled by chance.

You who felt a void before
toss your hats, cry for joy.
Fire has replaced your void.
You believe this fire is yours —
this Olympic fire.

You lofted the Olympic torch,
brought it so close
the barren land caught fire
like fields of dry grain.

The barren earth turns what is sown.
Nature abhors a void. The torch still burns.
You only have to gaze so long on water and fire
to understand fire, too, rushes into a vacuum.

See how alien intent winds through your speech,
how foreign fire flows through you.

You say: It's not foreign. I own my fire.
This is not anger, rather a kind of love.

See, how we love you — our engorged heart is slaked in blood.
We'll save, we'll kill you, in the name of love.

*Translated from the Russian by
Kevin Vaughn and Maria Khotimsky*

from COLD

And a neighbor-lady the other day lost her glorious dog, Tita.
And now she stands and chews
a clump of snow in her palm.
And a hand without a glove
is red as a shame.
And this I saw, in the morning, walking out of my window.
Walk, hug my torso, as if I know your torso.
Walk as if a hand can console a human torso.
(Step away from me, you idiot, my neighbor-lady yells.)

*

I am unaware of the concept of neighbors
Their faces, strange,
I see in backyards, on the morning walk to work
on the evening walk from work
I see their faces.
(And my body to their eyes, my body, is snow)
Momentary beings, lungs
in snow
who can console snow, lungs?

*

To winter's narrow splinter
Of a street, to an idiot neighbor
And her idiot dog
We will now announce:
glory.
To quiet and naked branches of poplars
To faces also quiet
In winter's splinter

Of a wind, say:
glory.
To a voice you don't hear
The real
Voice, cold, cut from stone in
a bone:
glory.
To no one, unknown
One blue on white
And quiet that splinters
the winter:
glory.

Translated from the Russian by Katie Farris and Ilya Kaminsky

SHE SPEAKS

1

I'm fed up with my own fear
Tired of living in a pigsty
Garbage trucks don't come anymore
They fear gunfire
So much trash
It's just not right
Rusty cans
Brown rusty cans on white
Snow

Who will take them away if not us?
Are we supposed to live in a landfill?
We walk across the field like living targets
Picking up cans,
Putting them in trash bags,
Rusty cans
Wedding bands
Vests
Boxes
The crows' black bodies
These bodies our own
Scattered remains

Fed up with my own fear
Fear also reaches some kind of threshold
After which something new begins
A dance with rusty cans in a white field

Housecleaning
Laundry
Snuggling in our sleep

Up to a certain moment
When time flares up like paper
Then crumbles into bits of ash
But there's no more fear
Never again will there be
Fear

2

She speaks, lit by winter sunshine,
The picture smears, disappears
Now only static remains,
Her words peck me like crows,
Peck at my heart, fed up with my own fear
Fed up with my own fear
Fed up with my own fear,

In a field
Half-eaten
By shell craters
As if by smallpox

She stands
With a shovel
And a bag
Full of trash

An interview
A blue microphone

Fed up with my own fear

Life beyond fear
Fearlessness on the verge of death

Translated from the Russian by Olga Livshin and Andrew Janco

* * *

On TV the news showed
a cat who birthed four kittens
five paws, seven noses
four tails with eyes so wide
they droop to their toes.

On TV they also said
we have it all,
two men down, three wounded,
unlimited gold in the ground.

It sits, spread in even yellow layers
that won't sparkle in the sun,
nor get melted into rings and wedding bands,
it remains silent; it's not for sale.

The gold has no voice, nor signals,
won't respond to heartfelt appeals,
settled so deep, no one will ever know
how immense it is, like a true secret.

On TV they don't mention it —
the situation inside the earth,
nor the situation beyond the conversation.
There will be no commentaries —
Absolutely none.

Translated from the Russian by
Kevin Vaughn and Maria Khotimsky

from THE PLAIN SENSE OF THINGS

1
Of simple things — whisper, whisper — not
touching the ear of another —
believe — in another's — eardrum.
So February opens, opens —
The time
whistles in a straw
as if a child sips from a glass of sparkling water.
Mouth opens, opens
before each word.
And the "o" of the mouth
is quiet
with want. Wide, and restrained, want.

3
And the snow comes as if no one knows about us
and no one needs us
and there was no
breath, no failure
and no earth that takes us inside.

9
Of simple things — in whisper, whisper.
So gives us to our bodies, time.
So the hands are held in hands, the bodies
drop into us.
So, the flame —
which comes from this evening
which is in our stomachs.

Our stomach, a city where we
are not yet persons. And no longer a breath, us.
And we — we want to go back to that breath, us.
We remember, us.

12
Of simple things whisper, whisper.
Whisper us. Us, time.

Translated from the Russian by Katie Farris and Ilya Kaminsky

* * *

1

That's my home.
There was a bridge here.
Now there isn't.

That's my home.
That's my yard.
It's still here.

Where a bridge stood,
there's a river.
No more bridge.

Where there was once a pass,
now there's a line.

We live here,
on the line.

In the devil's belly,
that's where.

2

I came back
Barely made it
Took a while to get everyone out
I have a big family
My parents are old
Then there are my

Brother my sister my
pregnant daughter
I got them all out
Out of that damned house
Just imagine
There's a river
There was a bridge there
Now it's destroyed
On the one side of the river these people
On the other side, those
Whoever they are
Between them, our house
It took me so many trips
There and back
For each person
I barely got them out
A big family
These on the one side, those on the other
The house stands like a shadow
As though lead passes through the walls
Or the house contorts its beams
So that it can dodge the hail of bullets
It twists left and right
What it took me, a woman
To get all of them out
You can't imagine
One by one
Right from the belly of the beast
Coming back every time,
Diving into all of that,
Not knowing
If there will be a way
But I got them all out

And now my daughter
Yes, the pregnant one
Says she wants to return
She's headed back tomorrow
She has someone there
A man she loves
See, he stayed back there
And love, well
You know how love goes
With those young people
You know how it is for them
Anything for love

Translated from the Russian by Olga Livshin and Andrew Janco

* * *

Can there be poetry after:
Yasynuvata, Horlivka, Savur-Mohyla, Novoazovsk
After:
Krasnyi-Luch, Donetsk, Luhansk
After
Sorting bodies in repose from the dying
The hungry from those on a stroll
Long after
Poetry devolves to "autistic babbling"
Lips mating in the darkness
I ask
Half-awake
Is poetry possible
At the moment history stirs
Once its steps
Reverberate through every heart?
Impossible to speak of anything else,
Talking becomes impossible.

As I write this
Very close to me
Every hope is being ended.

*Translated from the Russian by
Kevin Vaughn and Maria Khotimsky*

VASYL
HOLOBORODKO

NO RETURN

To come home means more than to be present
in the land I've left for a long time,
(you could come back in your thoughts as well),
but to truly return is to learn anew
the names of all things around you:
I stand under a pear tree laden with fruit,
elongated, like small jugs,
although it's not some cultivar,
rather an ordinary wild pear
whose name doesn't spring to mind,
I can only recall it as a special one.
What I can remember:
this pear tree bearing hard little "bony pears,"
languishing on the ground,
"lazy bones" or "rotties" as some called them.
What these pretty ones are,
I can't recall,
I ask an old neighbor:
he can't help me either,
just a pear, he says, that's it
but I know it carries its own name,
and I can't recall it
however hard I try,
standing here beneath this tree
laden with such small
elongated pears like little jugs.

(Epiphany: a
the name-no-name of the pear —
a symbol, by definition, of:
"something constant.")

Translated from the Ukrainian by Svetlana Lavochkina

I FLY AWAY IN THE SHAPE OF A DANDELION SEED

I know that from here you cannot escape by plane —
you have to be able to fly on your own.
Cats in the house, so many cats,
gathered from the whole neighborhood
(how did they catch a whiff of my departure?)
not our cats but feral cats,
although there is no such a thing as a cat gone wild.
Cats as a warning and threat to my flight
as a bird,
they notice a red spot on my chest
like a linnet's,
so I'm forced to take flight in the form of a dandelion seed:
I leave the house in search of wide open spaces,
past my garden and into the street
and float toward
a direction very remote —
now the wind gusts will
carry me away, away!

Translated from the Ukrainian by Svetlana Lavochkina

THE DRAGON HILLFORTS

All over Ukraine,
around every town and village
high walls jut from the landscape,
legend calls them serpents.

Pottery historians — archaeologists — study
where they belong
even radiocarbon dating
can't specify their age;
if we cannot determine a date —
if we cannot fathom the age of the hillforts,
they must have been here
as long as the Ukrainians.

Those walls are called serpents because
once upon a time
the holy blacksmiths Kuzma and Demian
harnessed a dragon to a plough;
this tillage jutted into the Serpent's Wall.
What else could have ploughed these forts but a dragon!

Epiphany:
a dragon — no-dragon —
a symbol, by definition, of:
"someone who possesses great power."

The hillforts were built to protect
against the cold creeping in from the forest,
so some people believe,
or for protection against

raw meat eaters from the forest,
so others believe,
or for protection against
invaders from the forest,
so the third party believes.

But no, dragon ploughing did not raise those hillforts,
our grandfathers wrapped them
around every town and village
to protect the dragon
from the cold given off by the forest,
from the raw meat eaters of the forest,
from the invaders lurking in the forest.

Epiphany:
dragon — no-dragon —
a symbol, by definition, of:
"someone who wields great power
whose purpose is to observe our Custom."

So rising all over Ukraine,
encircling every town and village
lofty hillforts,
dragon hillforts,
still protect our Dragon,
still protect our Custom.

Every year, the hillforts grow taller,
not because we, with every hatful, build them up little by little.
but because the graves of warriors force them upward,
defenders of our Dragon,
defenders of our Custom

buried in the hillforts,
around each town and village.

When I die,
bury me in a dragon hillfort,
so that the dragon hillforts around our Ukraine
grow taller by the thickness of the sheet of paper
on which this poem was written.

Translated from the Ukrainian by Svetlana Lavochkina

I PICK UP MY FOOTPRINTS

I stoop to pick up my footprints,
somebody seeing me might think
I'm gathering mushrooms,
healing herbs,
or flowers into a bunch,
but no —
I collect my footprints,
my traces everywhere
I walked for many years:
Here are the footprints I left while herding sheep on the steppe.
Here, I took this path to school,
and these are my steps from my route to work.

"I'm gathering my footprints here
so that strangers don't trample them,"
I tell anyone who's curious.

(Epiphany:
a footprint is —
a symbol, by definition, of:
"something rooted in the past")

In my mind, I slip my footprints
between the pages —
now whenever I read a book,
I chance upon an old footprint:
I study it for a long time,
the footprint I left as a child
walking beneath a cherry tree.

All the footprints gathered so far,
an entire footstep herbarium in books —
if I put them all in one row,
their path wouldn't lead me home.

Translated from the Ukrainian by Svetlana Lavochkina

BORYS
HUMENYUK

* * *

Our platoon commander is a strange man
When the sun rises over the battlefield
He says that it's someone burning a tire at a far-off checkpoint
The moon to him is a barrel of a cannon
And the sea is melted lead
Why is it salty?
Because it's made of our tears sweat piss blood
It flows through us.

A strange man, I say.
But today he outdid himself
In the early morning, he entered our tent and said
That's it! No more war today!
That's what they announced on TV —
War is done for three whole days.

Here at the front we've learned
There are two kinds of people: people, and TV people
We dislike TV people
They seem fake, they're poor actors
Actually, we don't even have TV
And if we did, we'd just watch cartoons (more truthful)
Or "In the World of Animals" (more interesting).

We were getting our weapons and ammo ready
When our weird platoon commander
Shocked us with this news.

The machine gun belt froze in the hands of gunner Vasyl
                                        from Kremenets
And his loader Sashko from Boyarka
Then it bristled, like the back of a prehistoric beast
The hand grenades peeking out of the pouch

Of grenadier Max from Luhansk
Dove back in like scared kittens.

Have you ever tried stopping a high-speed train
By placing a penny on the tracks?
Have you ever told the sun, wait, don't move
I've so much to do today.
Have you ever begged a woman in labor:
We've been snowed in, the midwife can't make it.
Hold on for three more days?

The child must be born
The train must reach its destination
The sun must keep rolling like a burning tire
And when it's gone the moon will take its place
As a cannon barrel
And night will fall as ash.

On the first day of no war
We lost our machine gun loader
Sashko from Boyarka
And grenadier Max from Luhansk
The bullets came from the other side of war
Like angry hornets
Stung Sashko in the neck
And Max in the heart
Maybe the other side doesn't have a strange platoon commander
Bringing weird news
Maybe they watch a different TV channel
Maybe their TV set is broken.

Translated from the Ukrainian by
Oksana Maksymchuk and Max Rosochinsky

* * *

These seagulls over the battlefield —
They are so ominous
I can understand ravens
They've long fed on the flesh of warriors.
They don't care whose flesh
Whether that of our heroes or our enemies.
I don't know if it pays to get mad at ravens
Even if it pains me to think of them

I can also understand pigeons
They're accustomed to rummaging through human trash
Even when they happen to use hair
They pulled from bloody shot-through skulls
To line their nests with
I understand them

I can understand sparrows
They simply want to eat
With a joyful chirping
They peck from the pockets and backpacks of the dead
Touching the eyes only by chance
Bits and pieces of bread cookies sugar coffee
And anything else the sparrows can take
As trophies
No longer needed by the dead

I understand sparrows
But begrudge the seagulls

They circle the field of the dead
Pink at dawn and dusk —

I try to tell myself that it's the light that turns them pink
Not blood
Flamingos turn pink
From eating shrimp
Seagulls can't turn pink so quickly
From eating the flesh of the dead
To achieve such an effect
The war must last over a year

They circle over the battlefield
Where no one remembers how to plow
How to build a home
How to sow grain
How to give birth to children

They circle the field
Dive down
Grab their prey
And they fly to the sea past our checkpoints
They get into scuffles
And sometimes drop their prey
Pieces of human flesh and bone fall to our feet
The awful thing is that we can't know —
If it's the flesh of friend or foe

It's uncanny to see
A human finger
Or an ear
Fall before you
From the sky.

Sometimes I think
That if you collect all the pieces

You might be able to put together a person —
Friend or enemy —
If only we could find someone to bring him back to life

Pink seagulls —
I wish I'd never seen them —
The greatest horror of this war
Along with those pieces of human flesh
That fall from the sky
And you have no idea what to do with them
You can't dig a grave for just one
Torn off finger.

Translated from the Ukrainian by
Oksana Lushchevska and Michael M. Naydan

* * *

When HAIL rocket launchers are firing
Over residential neighborhoods
Be they Lebanese, Syrian, or Georgian
Or those in Mariupol, Artemivsk, Antratsyt —
There is something normal about it,
But of course only as much as HAIL
Rockets firing are normal

It's normal when HAIL fire balls
Hit nurseries
Where children are sleeping
It's normal when they strike
Supermarkets full of people
Railway stations and airports
It's normal when civilians die
By hundreds and thousands
Because it's normal when civilians
Die in war — but of course
Only as much as war itself is normal

It's normal that children run to playgrounds
Where they find blood-spattered toys of children
Who were taken to the morgue yesterday —
Kids being kids —
They clutch the blood-spattered toys
Parents attempt to pry the toys away
The children cry
Our toys are not as nice.
And this is normal.
Just so normal.

It's normal that feeble old women
whose families left them to care for their homes
when they fled to escape the war —
Because it's war here —
After three days stuck in a basement
Without water or food
Choose the ablest and youngest
Send her to the nearest water pump
with two three-gallon plastic drums.
The brave old woman was returning
When they saw through a crack
A shell explode, tearing off her leg.
Then another old woman crawled from the basement
And took the canisters from her
Saying "I'm sorry, Valia,"
Then crawled back to safety.
It's normal —
All too normal.

It's normal when a veteran obstetrician —
A dried-eyed atheist —
Who operated on the entire Majdan
Goes to church, lights a candle
Falling to her knees, crying
Lord, spare us this war
For the second month in a row
Only baby boys

It's normal for people to die in war —
When war itself is impossible to avoid
Impossible to fly over even in a "Boeing"
At a very high altitude.
Impossible to sit it out.

It's normal when a shell drops on a cemetery,
levels the graves of our parents.
It's normal when soldiers dig trenches
and build bunkers there.
The cemetery is strategically located
We will never know who ends up buried in those trenches.
This is the war of all against all —
It touches everyone —
The dead, the living, and those not yet born.

But what's unnatural is when a shell
Fired from a HAIL rocket launcher
Accidentally strikes a field.
It's unnatural to watch
Unharvested rye burning,
To listen to ground squirrels cry
While mice scurry in every direction
As the fire and the war
Catch and swallow them.
Because fire and war are unquenchable.

It's unnatural to watch
Quails circle their nests
Nestlings crying for help
Growing silent one by one
Consumed by the fire.

But you feel truly sorry for the quails.
Because people make war.
Quails don't make war.
Quails are not to blame for anything.

Translated from the Ukrainian by
Oksana Lushchevska and Michael M. Naydan

* * *

Not a poem in forty days
Poetry went to the grave
When on November 23rd
Andriy Yurga, a fighter of the "OUN" battalion
Died in battle at Pisky
He came from Lviv, nickname "Davyd."

Poetry turned black
Wore mourning clothes for forty days
Then it was covered with earth
Then with ash
Forty days poetry sat in the trenches
Clenching its teeth shooting back in silence
Poetry didn't want to talk to anyone
What is there to talk about?
Death?

During those forty days poetry saw many deaths.

Poetry saw trees die.
Those that ran through the minefields of a fall
And never made it to winter.

Poetry saw animals die.
Wounded cats and dogs
Dragging their spilling guts down the streets
As if this were something ordinary
Poetry didn't know what to do:
Take pity and help them die, or
Take pity and let them live.

Poetry saw houses die.
Their house,

your house.
Was that *your* house
over there, around the corner?

A year ago, an ordinary house
With flowers in the front
And a garden in the back,
With apple trees, plum trees, pear trees,
A walnut tree in the garden
With the people that used to
Live there.

When the first bullet came
The house didn't understand
It gasped quietly
And wept quietly:
The bullet wounded a wall.

Other bullets came
The house could never guess when they would arrive
It couldn't get ready for them
Cover itself with hands
Hide in the attic or
in the basement.

The bullets made holes in the walls
broke the windows
They flew into the house
the kitchen, the living room,
The kids' room.
Looking for people.
Bullets always look for people.

People are the reason for a house.

Then came the mortar shell
In autumn, the house used to like the sound
of walnuts and apples
hitting the roof.
Now the shell hit the roof.

Then came a rocket from the rocket launcher.
The house leapt up like a girl
Jumping over a fire at the summer solstice
It hung in the air for a moment
then landed slowly
but it could no longer stand up straight.
Walls, floors, furniture,
kids toys, kitchenware, grandfather clock,
all of it bitten by war,
licked by fire.

Poetry saw people die.
Poetry put spent bullet shells in its ears.
Poetry would rather go blind
than see corpses every day.

Poetry is the shortcut to heaven.
Poetry sees into the void.
When you fall
It lets you remember your way back.
Poetry went places
where there isn't place for poetry.

Poetry witnessed it all.
Poetry witnessed it all.

Translated from the Ukrainian by
Oksana Maksymchuk and Max Rosochinsky

* * *

An old mulberry tree near Mariupol
Has never seen so many boys in her life
Boys picking her fruit, boys dancing in the branches,
And the smallest boy climbing
To the very top.

RPGs, a machine gun, sniper rifles, helmets, bullet-proof vests
All laid carefully down.

The boys laughed, gave each other piggyback rides,
Smeared mulberry juice all over their faces
Sometimes on purpose — to look
like characters from Hollywood movies.

RPGs, a machine gun, sniper rifles, helmets, bullet-proof vests
All laid carefully down.

Beyond the horizon some mortars went to work
Making a funny noise: "one, two, three," "one"
Like a young lover knocking on a girl's window.
A flock of ravens rose into the sky with a shriek
But maybe those weren't ravens, maybe
Those were airborne clumps of earth, tilled by the explosions.

The boys abandoned the old mulberry tree
Left it whirling in a solitary dance
Changed into grown men.
They sped off to assume their positions
Beyond the horizon, where the earth cried out to the sky
And the sky shook.

The old mulberry tree
Is waiting for her boys by the road
But nobody comes to pick her fruit.
It falls to the ground like bloody tears.

The grass that was pressed beneath
The RPGs, a machine gun, sniper rifles, helmets, bullet-proof vests
All straightened out.

And when the moon rises in the sky
The old mulberry tree
Gets on her tiptoes, like a girl
Tries to peek over the horizon
Where are you, boys?

Translated from the Ukrainian by
Oksana Maksymchuk and Max Rosochinsky

* * *

When you clean your weapon
When time and again, you clean your weapon
When you rub strong-smelling oils into your weapon
And shield it from the rain with your own body
When you swaddle it like a baby
Even though you've never swaddled a baby before —
You're only nineteen, no baby, no wife —
The weapon becomes your only kin
You and the weapon are one.

When you dig trench after trench
When you dig this precious this hateful earth by handfuls
Every other handful reaches your soul
You grind this earth between your teeth
You don't, you never will have another
You climb into the earth like into your mother's womb
You are warm and snug
You've never felt this close to anyone before
You and earth are one.

When you shoot
Even when it's at night and you don't see the enemy's face
Even when night hides the enemy from you and you from the enemy
And embraces each of you as her own
You smell like gunpowder
Your hands, face, hair, clothing, shoes —

No matter how much you wash them — smell of gunpowder
They smell of war
You smell of war
You and war are one.

Translated from the Ukrainian by
Oksana Maksymchuk and Max Rosochinsky

A TESTAMENT

Today we are digging the earth again
This hateful Donetsk earth
This stale, petrified earth
We press ourselves into it
We hide in it
Still alive

We hide behind it
Sit silently in it
Like little children behind their mother's back
We hear its heart beating
Its weary breath
We are warm and comfortable
Still alive

Tomorrow we will die
Maybe some of us
Maybe all of us

Don't take us from the earth
Don't tear us away from our mother

Don't gather our remains from the field
Don't try to put us back together again
And — we beg you — don't erect crosses
Monuments or memorial slabs
We don't need them
Because it isn't for us —
You erect these monuments for yourselves.

Don't engrave our names,
Simply remember:
On this field
In this earth
Ukrainian soldiers lie
And — that is all.

Don't return us to our parents
We don't want them to see us like this
Let our parents remember us children
Naughty little boys
With slingshots and bruised knees
With failing marks on their report cards
With shirts crammed with apples from the neighbor's orchard
Let our parents believe that we'll return one day
That we are somewhere

Don't return us to our wives
Let them remember us handsome
As men well-liked by women
Who belonged to their wives alone
Let them remember our warm kisses
Our loving embraces
Don't let them touch our cold foreheads
Our cold lips

Don't return us to our children
Let our children remember our kind eyes
Our kind smiles
Our kind hands
Don't let our children's lips
Touch our cold hands

In these trenches
Today our temporary homes
Tomorrow our graves
Bury us

We don't need eulogies
In the silence that follows battle.
They always seem odd —
Like punching a dead soldier
Then ordering him to his feet

We don't need funerals
We know where our place is
Simply cover us with earth
And move on

It would be nice if there was a field
Where rye is swaying
A lark flies overhead
And — the sky
The endless sky —
Can you imagine the grain a field
Where warriors are lying will yield?

To remember us, eat the grain from the field
Where we laid down our lives

It would be good if there were meadows there
And many flowers
And a bee under each flower
And lovers who come in the evening
To weave wreaths
To make love till dawn
And during the day, let new parents
Bring their young children
Don't keep children from coming to us

But this will be tomorrow
Today we are still digging the earth
This cherished Ukrainian earth
This sweet, gentle earth
And with a soldier's spade we write as one
On its body
The last Ukrainian poem of the last poets
Left alive

Translated from the Ukrainian by
Oksana Lushchevska and Michael M. Naydan

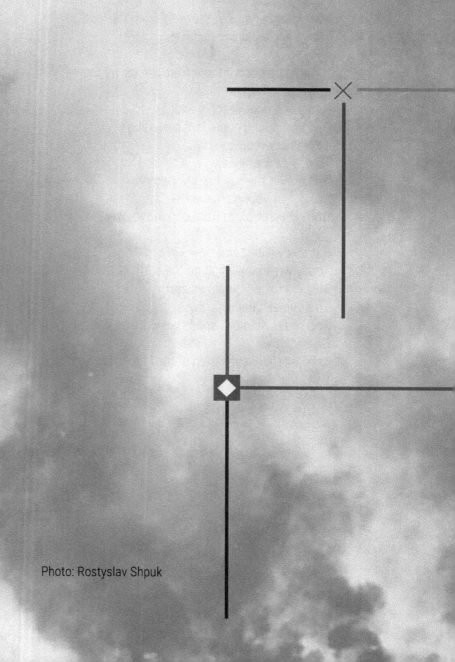

Photo: Rostyslav Shpuk

YURI
IZDRYK

DARKNESS INVISIBLE

evil has melted away in our world, as ice turns to water
diffused invisibly, like mist in air
grope in the deepest, darkest of pits, your search will be futile
you cannot say evil is here, evil is there

for its spores are dispersed in the pores of the earth, even and smooth
you can meet it at any old time, any old place
for evil is not a big lie, but small shards, resembling truth
its metastases glitter like crystals in each one of us

for evil inheres in the reader — not the Vedas, the Bible, or the Koran
evil can't lead, it lures — and each of us must decide
whether to go into battle, called by the beat of a drum
whether to head for the shimmering, coarse, bloody fraud

evil pleads for compassion, though it knows no compassionate ways
asks for a sacrifice, but won't give a penny to anyone
for evil delights at the sight of the littlest tear on your face
though it really regards others' tears as meaningless fun

just as black and white merge in a dance instead of a fray
just as prayer and profanity mingle within a gray din
evil can't be discerned — like death seeded in you and in me
evil has merged with the world — it's as if it were gone

while we two are together, I keep faith in light, love, and warmth
and in mercy, which conquers invisible darkness

the shadows will fade, evil will surface — pathetic, a thing of no worth
and we two will laugh, we'll laugh right in its face

Translated from the Ukrainian by Boris Dralyuk

MAKE LOVE

this war isn't war — it's a chance not to kill anyone
this love isn't love unto death — it's as long as it lasts
to protect one another is all this occasion demands
and to look at the world through a steady rifle sight
and to look within ourselves through every microscope
and to look at you at every hour every minute at all times
to protect one another — and in keeping calm and carrying on
to burn down to the ground and to rise up as smoke
this war isn't war — but a certain and fiery passion
this love is forever — just as moments pass forever
we hit bottom to get stuck in some new heaven
there is a string that binds us all together
that string between us is a safety fuse

Translated from the Ukrainian by Boris Dralyuk

Photo: Pavel Feinstein

ALEKSANDR
KABANOV

* * *

This is a post on Facebook, and this, a block post in the East,
our losses: the five banned, six shipped back "in zinc coffins,"
the wounded, everyone: the Ukes, the Ruskis, Merkel, verses.
God himself had been mined somewhere on lofty heights.

This summer, without bulletproof vest, in September, no helmet,
the trolling "Kuban" battalion against our couch centurions;
I'll make you a gift: a camouflage case for your tablet;
time is earwax, peddled in alleyways, under the table.

So when all is said and done, what did I do for this baby:
Stroked her nipples with a cursor, tickled her underarms?
'Cause she so wanted to get married, and now in revenge,
she'll suck off the recruiter and bring me my draft notice.

May the blessed relics rest in peace: her Lacoste t-shirt,
the high-speed Wi-Fi, all your likes and statuses reposted,
for the heroes never die. The heroes never die, this,
the very first roadblock at the besieged towers of Troy.

Translated from the Russian by Alex Cigale

* * *

How I love — out of harm's way.
How I love — at the margins of the law —
silence wrapped in furs, bedecked in bells,
dusty bellows of accordion.

Christmas time in a godforsaken desert,
some deserted snow covers the sand.
Orange shivers in its foxy pelt,
juicy grapes are rolling down the canvas.

Sadness withers, then it blooms again
as the berry of resentment ripens.
I'm in love, but Moscow is behind me,
tucked in tight into shahid's bomb belt.

Warsaw and Berlin are still before us.
Eunuchs and barbarians and goners
and a wedge of cranes that sadly clangs
in the delicate rice paper skies.

We're alone, and we are down by law,
smeared with blood, with guilt and fear.
We emerged from a great war.
Nothing small can make us disappear.

Translated from the Russian by
Oksana Maksymchuk and Max Rosochinsky

A FORMER DICTATOR

In a hat and sweatpants made of tinfoil
I go out on a terrace, having turned on the wire.
From the distance, I sense the stirrings of my foe.
Time to recharge my laser gun and fire.

The morning is beautiful, zero chance of rain.
Perfect time for a smoke, but I misplaced the matches.
Alpha-rays affect the tissue of the brain,
beta and gamma rays hit the heart and the testes.

My tinfoil protection clears frees me from fear.
It's too bad that my wardrobe has gotten so sparse.
I'm recalling the Bible — that R-rated verse
where the nameless author kills the hero,

then resurrects him, then robs him of hope.
What's for breakfast: a baby, a snail, or a tortoise.
The favorites on my iPad are really dope:
an album of interrogations that end in torture.

If I get served for breakfast some tender cops,
puffy ruffians, hitmen poached to perfection,
then I'll know that the rays messed me up
and I'll put on a tinfoil balaclava for protection.

Then I'll know that it's time to vanish, to disappear
in a dream, in Crimea. An angel pale as lard
sent to rescue me, gives me the middle finger
and I shoot it off — like an unwanted rhyme.

Translated from the Russian by
Oksana Maksymchuk and Max Rosochinsky

* * *

He came first wearing a t-shirt inscribed "Je suis Christ,"
a long-haired hippy, but in this Coming he was beardless,
on his neck, flowering like a December rose, was a hickey;
he'd developed problems with human relations, and nature.

He transformed the golden fish into black bread and wine,
and then again changed this new wine into moonshine:
in this way, a child who is not long for this world,
smashes the piggy-bank kitty for all eyes to see.

Like empty talk, the streetcar clangs off to the depot,
sounds throw shadows — longer, colder, more amorphous;
Indeed, Pasternak has risen, despite the weak Wi-Fi signal,
bringing us a joint for the road, heroin, and some morphine.

Translated from the Russian by Alex Cigale

* * *

In the garden of Gethsemane on the Dnieper river
where the baseball bats are in bloom
shrieks the two-headed ~~eagle~~ cockatoo:
the parachute turned out to be a balloon!

Our dacha community warden
opens up, helps us out at the gate.
He says that Maidan is over.
How many Maidans will it take?

Armillaria caps — oily stars —
light our way all the way until dawn.
Souls are moaning in Orthodox bonds
and the baseball bats are in bloom.

Human herds happily graze
to outlaw songs on the radio:
"I fell out of love with you, miss!
You're against the European Union."

Translated from the Russian by
Oksana Maksymchuk and Max Rosochinsky

* * *

A Russian tourist is on vacation
relaxing like a soldier before battle
tomorrow bayonets bullets
he can't fall back: behind him
executioners penal battalions

A Russian tourist is on vacation
in his head winter harsh
frost deer cloudberry Lower Tagil
have you ever lived in Lower Tagil?
even January prefers
Upper Tagil or Perm

A Russian tourist is on vacation
yet he doesn't forget to remind the Turks
of the Russo-Turkish War and Shipka
the Egyptians of the Aswan Dam
the Germans of the concentration camps
and just the fact that they're German

Vacation is political education
vodka is anesthesia
a Russian song is a forewarning
If you hear a moaning Swede
beaten up in the lobby
a shrieking Pole drowning in the pool
know that it's nothing: just a Russian tourist
a Russian tourist is on vacation

Translated from the Russian by
Oksana Maksymchuk and Max Rosochinsky

* * *

Fear is a form of the good,
an angelic portion.
Peter's cotton ball shadow
loses consciousness.

Bald, with a funny moustache,
he drinks plum brandy
until he finds his true self,
becoming — a dead man.

Sparrows read the last rites.
Mole crickets do the honors.
Horror — a symbol of love —
reeks of leftovers.

Like an explosive blast,
join the kids in the basement.
Life gets to all of us,
each one will catch a shard.

Glue sticks explode in the sky.
Oil tankers make us high.
Was it all worth a try,
wasn't it worth it?

Translated from the Russian by
Oksana Maksymchuk and Max Rosochinsky

* * *

Once upon a time, a Jew says to his prisoner, his Hellenic foe:
"I will never forgive, but get out of here, go back home,
tell the Achaean mothers how we crumbled up their brood,
how we like cooking up that kind of Greek food.

"Tell their fathers that the war of worlds, tongues, truths
turned into a farce, into the annexation of territory.
Here's some kebab and some genuine bullfinch booze,
here's a kick in the butt, Heracles, or what's your face, Gregory . . ."

. . . Beyond the olive grove, the mine workers' Hades is on fire
and the double sun rises without a face mask.
Ten years of truce. Who's that guy that salutes me, Nazi-style
"Glory to the Spartans!" with a thick Jewish accent?

"Girkinson, helmet down!" — I signal in response,
make it back to the camp just in time for a roll call.
At bedtime I pull a tablet out of my trendy trousers,
I browse the news, check my inbox.

There he goes again, that Jesus Christ,
talking as usual about peace, about universal love,
how he led the flock through the steppe to this land,
how his foes cornered him, placed a bounty on his head,
how they then crucified him on air, live
and now you can ask him a question over Skype.

Translated from the Russian by
Oksana Maksymchuk and Max Rosochinsky

KATERYNA KALYTKO

* * *

They won't compose any songs, because the children of their children,
hearing about this initiation, will jump out of their beds at 4 a.m.,
                                                                    frightened
by the echo in their spinal cords. Separate parts of death
cannot form a whole: a quarter of fate or of body is always missing.
The map is worn at the folds.

The doors of the house rust hopelessly, you are on night watch.
At dawn saliva becomes poison in every mouth.
All these piles of ashes still have names
and they keep repeating their persistent calls
sharp like panicked bird shrieks, too extreme for a song
about a field torn apart by a hail of bullets,
about the *chornozem* that God will rub off in his hand afterwards.

Translated from the Ukrainian by
Olena Jennings and Oksana Lutsyshyna

APRIL 6

You are not just sleeping with this one man, but with his whole life,
and sometimes it wakes you up and snatches him out of your arms.
For, you see, war often comes along and lies down between you
                                                    like a child
afraid to be left alone in the dark.

War, he says, involves many numbers, let's see —
two relatives equal one sack of bones,
one thousand three hundred ninety-five days of siege,
three packages of humanitarian aid: butter, canned goods,
                            powdered milk, three bars of soap.

Four armed men come for you,
show you their orders and then escort you out into the night.
During the walk across the city
you hear missiles flying over your head — twice.

. . . Five times they take you out of the barracks
to a ditch where forty-three lay rotting
and each time you think: I will finally die
and tell God that it was a lame joke.

But they throw you face down into the dirt
and take their sweet time pressing a gun to your head.
Since then, he says, I don't like to dream,
these kinds of memories, they aren't fitting for a man.

You run through the woods, they shoot at your back,
a bullet hits your thigh but all you feel is this dirt on your face.
That's when a leafless tree of pain grows
in your chest, pulsating.

And I don't respond because what do you say to that
I just keep wiping the dirt off his face, over and over again,
even while he's sleeping,
even while he's away.

*Translated from the Ukrainian by
Olena Jennings and Oksana Lutsyshyna*

* * *

This loneliness could have a name, an Esther or a Miriam.
Regiments fall to the ground with an infant's cry.
Words hardly fit between water and salt.
Under the flag at half-mast, hundreds of hoarse voices

laugh, pricked by the splinters of language.
This loneliness is vast, bottomless, and so chilling
that even a stranger turns away. Restless children wander
out of the school, stand by the sea, as if in front of a tribunal.

Dried tree branches crackle in the air like transmitters.
Somebody keeps calling out the name of the city turned into ashes.
This loneliness could be named Sevgil or Selima.
The names of the abandoned are salty and deep.

She comes out, fumbles with the knot
of her black headscarf; her lips are pale.
Who is there, she says, do you read me? Does anyone hear us?
Just a moment ago somebody called out our names.

Do you read me, son, try and listen to me, to me —
they have all left the shore, look for them in the sea.

Translated from the Ukrainian by
Olena Jennings and Oksana Lutsyshyna

* * *

Home is still possible there, where they hang laundry out to dry,
and the bed sheets smell of wind and plum blossoms.
It is the season of the first intimacy
to be consummated, never to be repeated.
Every leaf emerges as a green blade
and the cries of life take over the night and find a rhythm.

Fragile tinfoil of the season when apricots first form
along with wars and infants, in the same spoonful of air,
in the stifling bedrooms or in the cold, from which the wandering
beg to enter, like a bloom of jellyfish, or migratory blossoms.
The April frost hunts white-eyed, sharp-clawed,
but the babies have the same fuzzy skin for protection.

What makes them different is how they break
when the time comes for them to fall, or if they get totally crushed.
Behind the wall a drunken one-armed neighbor stumbles around his
                                                              house,
confusing all the epochs, his shoulder
bumps into metal crutches from WWI, a Soviet helmet made of
                                                       cardboard,
and the portrait of a man with a glance like a machine gun firing
and hangers for shirts, all of them with a single sleeve.

So they will fall and break into pieces and fates
branches parted, fruit exposed to the winds.
The neck feels squeezed, in the narrow isthmus of the throat
time just stands still and mustard gas creeps through the ditches.
All of this is but a forgotten game we play in the family backyard,
hiding amongst the laundry that hangs outside
the world becomes more fragile at each moment, and when you
                                              suddenly embrace

through the cloth — you don't know who it is, and whether you've lost
.or found.

And the swelling parted body of war intrudes into a blossoming heart
because we didn't let it enter our home on a cold night to warm itself.

Translated from the Ukrainian by
Olena Jennings and Oksana Lutsyshyna

HE WRITES

They were disliked on earth and forsaken among the clouds.
Yuri Andrukhovych

Mother, you haven't sent me a single photograph
so I almost forgot what your face looks like.
You'll cry, I know, I have caused you distress
but each trouble is just a tiny speck of blood
on a Sunday dress.

Life is a house on the side of the road,
old-world style, like our peasant house, divided into two parts.
In one, they wash the dead man's body and weep.
In the other, they dress a bride.

Mother, I want you to have a dream in which I come
and sit in the part with more light.

You cry so much mother, you don't stop sobbing.
I can't see your face well, but faces don't matter much,
Your hair, I still remember, smells of cornflowers.

They all want something from us and keep stirring
the anthill of the army, in which the country lies like a rotting fish.
I wrote to Andrew, a long soulful letter,
but didn't get a reply, maybe I got the address wrong.

And before that Andrew wrote: how he remembers the taste of
the toffee that Dad used to bring from town, also the slippery ravine

behind our house. Peter, he wrote, if we ever return, it will be
on stretchers.
Mother was right — we should have remained fishermen.

Rain drums loudly, mud covers the front lines.
We march hopelessly along rivers and under the clouds.
I'm forgetting everything, as if memories were leaking out of me.
. . . Mother, does that girl Hafiya still sing in the church choir?

Translated from the Ukrainian by
Olena Jennings and Oksana Lutsyshyna

* * *

Can great things happen to ordinary people?
The rotting boards of knowledge creak underfoot.
Now you know, for example, how in wartime
lights pulsate on Christmas trees in squat homes,
how the deadly wind blows from a burning field
burrowing like a stent between aorta walls
how Gaspar, Balthazar, Melchior
rush in an ambulance with a bullet-riddled headlight
how the thick magic forests appear out of compassion for the
                                        prisoners of war
and spread in a layer of peat over the darkened souls.
Daylight, a clawing puppy, whimpers by the pillow,
the light is faint and snowy, snow will cool the faces
and capture them turning into icon-like images
that cut through the heart of the earth.

If there is no warmth
until spring, let this shroud remain.
Was everything, everything that happened, for a greater good
or would all the agony cause a tall tree to grow — bleeding
berries, pounding against apartment windows at night?
Where did you get this glistening moonlight skin, my love?
From starvation, despair, and milk, and mercury.

Translated from the Ukrainian by
Olena Jennings and Oksana Lutsyshyna

LYUDMYLA
KHERSONSKA

* * *

Did you know that if you hide under a blanket and pull it over your head,
then, for sure, World War II won't happen? Instead,
lie there don't breathe, don't let your feet stick out,
or, if you do, stick one out bit by bit.
Or try this helpful trick to stop a war:
first, carefully stick out one foot, then the other, now touch the floor,
lie back down, turn to one side, facing the wall,
turn your back to the war:
now that it's behind your back, it can thrash and shred,
you just close your eyes, pull the blanket over your head, stock up
on bread,
and when you just can't deal with caring for peace anymore,
tear off some chunks, and when the night comes, eat what
you've stored.

Translated from the Russian by Olga Livshin and Andrew Janco

* * *

How to describe a human other than he's alone —
what to add that he himself won't guess to add?
Pockets full of posies? A little lamb for Mary?
What else is there to cast at a man?

A human is alone whether he dies or
snores. What else to say about a sleeping man?

A man is sleeping or simply turned to a wall?
A man turned to a wall not to see his nation.

Another turned to a wall between four walls,
a man who turned to a wall, weary of war.
Ear of the war: so much noise from a single man,
as if a whale was birthed into a common shell,
as if fear was trapped in the heart's punchbag.
A lonely human is dust,
where to run from dust?
Where the nose points? But a person needs lunch.
A roof over his head, a sun over his head, and also to laugh.
Blood over his head, and also to bleed,
one man for all man.
No man for one man. Anybody? No one.

A man in trouble, in death, in office, in line,
in vogue, in disguise, in fight: everywhere alone.
A brown-haired man, a redhead, a blond,
a white man, a black man, a rainbow-man,
one person: singled red with sorrow, by one wall.

Translated from the Russian by Valzhyna Mort

* * *

The whole soldier doesn't suffer —
it's just the legs, the arms,
just blowing snow,
just meager rain.
The whole soldier shrugs off hurt —
it's just missile systems "Hail" and "Beech,"
just bullets on the wing,
just happiness ahead.
Just meteorological pogroms,
geo-Herostratos wannabes,
just the girl with the pointer
poking the map in the stomach.
Just thunder, lightning,
just dreadful losses,
just the day with a dented helmet,
just God, who doesn't protect.

Translated from the Russian by Katherine E. Young

* * *

A country in the shape of a puddle, on the map.

Any country is an easy target in March,
in June, July, August, September, October,
as long as it rains
and maps litter the street.

Stop, who goes there, General Oaken Knees.
The Red Square of his naked chest shines the way.
And behind him, a half-shadow, half-man,
half-orphan, half-exile, whose mouth is as coarse
as his land —
                double-land where every cave is at war.

Do you say there won't be a war? I say nothing.

A small gray person cancels
this twenty-first century,
adjusts his country's clocks
for the winter war.

Translated from the Russian by Valzhyna Mort

* * *

Buried in a human neck, a bullet looks like an eye, sewn in,
an eye looking back at one's fate.
Who shot him there? Who gave the order, which man?
Who will bury him, and what's the rate?
When it comes to humanity, war is the beginning and end.
Whoever attacks you, don't turn your back.
Says the Lord: For my people are foolish, they have not known me,
they are silly children and they have no understanding.
But the children feel as strong as their machinery,
mass-produced, with plenty of seamstresses for repairing:
some ladies patch holes, others fix neck bones,
still more sew on buttons that were torn away from hands.
And the Lord says: They are wise in doing evil — but,
says the Lord — they do not know how to do good.
But the children, if they survive, say it was luck,
and if they die, they think that was yesterday,
today is another day,
and the seamstresses stand with a shroud, telling them, "Put this on."
How long must we put up with the flags, the trumpets calling
us into the fray?
What beast has awakened? Where did our special forces land?
Who shot that man in the back? Who gave the command?
Who will bury him, and what's the rate?

Translated from the Russian by Olga Livshin and Andrew Janco

* * *

that's it: you yourself choose how you live,
whose hand to shake,
for whom the bell tolls, for whom you grieve,
whom you'll run to save.
as in a solfège class, you're the one who listens,
picks out the false note, conducts *one-two-three*.
you lift up your head — flocks of angels sail the heavens,
cranes in v-formation, see.
life passed without war, war passed to the side,
but forgot something, left it, turned back mid-stride.
then you yourself choose how you'll handle war,
you select the weather — hurricane, hail?
you slam the window closed.
all this was long ago . . .

Translated from the Russian by Katherine E. Young

* * *

I planted a camellia in the yard.
I wanted to be a lady, not a war-ravaged rag,
to cast down my lashes, let fall a light glove,
put on red beads, patent-leather boots,
I listen: are there explosions,
does someone stomp the earth . . .

Translated from the Russian by Katherine E. Young

* * *

One night, a humanitarian convoy arrived in her dream.
Legs drawn to her chest, head under the sheet,
she sleeps on her right side, back braced by the wall,
the way people sleep during humanitarian wars.
The same exact way all tribes sleep at all times,
waking only because of silence, that awful silence,
during that silence, don't open the gates —
behind them, little humanitarians, heads facing the wrong way.

Translated from the Russian by Katherine E. Young

* * *

When a country of — overall — nice people
turns — slowly — fascist,
nice people do not notice this transformation all at once.

As when a person we know intimately
goes, next to us, through
an imperceptible process of aging. Imperceptibly, new wrinkles
slice the skin, frightening, deep.

Nice people nod when they run into each other,
and try, more and more, to lower their eyes,

until finally, raising them becomes an inhuman gesture.

Translated from the Russian by Valzhyna Mort

* * *

Leave me alone, I'm crying. I'm crying, let me be.
Our peace-loving neighbor is fixing his peaceful roof,
patching leaks caused by April showers, HAIL rockets.
Me, I'm crying about the cat's skin lesions, about me
when I was little. As if grownups needed further proof
they are always right, the kitty has to stay outside, the door is locked.
She is crying out in the rain, I can hear her. Rain feels like hell
to her. To run outside barefoot, to grab the shocked,
heavy-furred, wet-eyed cat — then run back — see,
Mom won't let me. I am crying, just let me be.
In peacetime, in childhood time, a child has her own hell
when the cat — who has sores — isn't home.
We are crying, me and the cat, and everyone leaves us alone.
A little refugee girl from Donetsk: I'll build a house for the cat,
if you have a home, you don't get sick and you don't sneeze.
To save one life, one living life, even a cat's life.
But rain is hard to explain to the cat
and how would you explain the war? — she says, sighing, to me.
Such a big girl. Leave me alone, I'm crying.

Translated from the Russian by Olga Livshin
and Andrew Janco

* * *

the enemy never ends,
he's just trouble, just trouble
that spreads like lichen on the brain,
like moss underfoot,
the enemy's there, where your own folk are offended,
where they're humbled,
the enemy's there, where you can't keep quiet.
the place you wanted to explore, protect, shield,
that's where the enemy appears, plants his hoof in the earth,
to that hoof, all living things are just blood, death, earth.
from kremlin to kremlin
to Crimea itself, to Crimea
stretches moss, moss, moss,
but the enemy says cross, cross, cross
and people shrug their shoulders, turn aside, and walk right by

Translated from the Russian by Katherine E. Young

* * *

every seventh child of ten — he's a shame
to give up on, but troublesome to maintain —
digs a pit for the next, who can't be saved.

the brothers who remain — nine little Indians —
all want to stay alive, yet want to kill,
and doing what they want, pitch into that pit.

every teenage moron who goes to class
mocks the teacher sideways, then to his face,
every teenage moron, he hates your ass.

for every moron there's a diploma, photo,
certificate, paid vacation, doctor's note,
but what he really loves: when things explode.

every fool who can, grips his gun tight,
refuses to give up, dives into the fight —
who goes there, halt — oaths crackle, flare, ignite.

whom do you want to shoot? who goes there, halt!
heartsick, knife in your brother's back, yawn
of the pit — you don't want to, but in you fall.

Translated from the Russian by Katherine E. Young

* * *

you really don't remember Grandpa — but let's say you do.
he walked on one leg, because the other leg
came unbuckled and lay nights on the bed's edge
watching over the room, many rooms.
when you're a youngster, short and small,
when every large object seems to be Grandpa
— you really don't remember Grandpa — Grandpa's always
coming closer, closer in winter than in summer.

Translated from the Russian by Katherine E. Young

BORIS
KHERSONSKY

* * *

explosions are the new normal, you grow used to them
stop noticing that you, with your ordinary ways, are a goner
a trigger man and a sapper wander around the park
whispering like a couple — I wish I could eavesdrop

surely, it goes this way: where there's a shovel, there's a tunnel
where there's a conspiracy, there's a catch
where there's God, there's a threshold
stalky Ukrainians — where granny tends to a garden patch

surely it's about the meaning of death, sudden as a mudslide
surely it's about the vodka: to relieve mortal anguish
once you've shown you have any brain, they'll brain you hard into
submission
hair impeccably parted — where you spot a geometrically neat
moustache

a trigger man and a sapper wander around like a couple
as the angel of destruction observes them tenderly from the cloud
we're captive birds dear brother that's it that's all
black sun of melancholy shines like a shrapnel hole

Translated from the Russian by Ostap Kin
and Polina Barskova

* * *

all for the battlefront which doesn't really exist
all for victory which will never come, but still
all for the dusty paths for distant planets
all for those in the future and in the past

all for those who came before us, who will follow us
who will reap what we sow, repeat our favorite blunders
so that we don't get as much as a single crumb
so that we the living don't get a single drop

Translated from the Russian by Ostap Kin
and Polina Barskova

* * *

people carry explosives around the city
in plastic shopping bags and little suitcases
they trample the cobblestone we learn their secrets
only the day after and even then it's just checking the facts

how many windows shattered how many collapsed balconies
did anyone die or is everyone alive and kicking
only frightened that there is no more peaceful life perhaps
war happens and the laws of war are a cruel thing

or perhaps there are no more laws and explosions are now the norm
we don't get up from the table just shiver and shed some hope
an enemy chooses weapons as a thief finds the pick for a door
when in fact the door is already open

Translated from the Russian by Olga Livshin
and Andrew Janco

* * *

way too long the artillery and the tanks stayed silent in their hangars
way too long the rockets stood waiting and aimed in their shafts
way too long children slept peacefully and students grew bored at lectures
discussing their professors, all of them bureaucrats and old farts

way too long supermarket shelves sagged with goods
way too long beautiful women rolled their carts along the aisles
way too long wolves didn't show their fangs in the Briansk woods
way too long the enemies of the people went unsupervised

someone wrote of the end of history,
that it stopped its flow, rarely waking up, joking out of boredom
and where are you, the heroes of the front and the heroines of the
                                                          hinterlands
battling the burdens of separation at the conveyor belts

the art of war had been lost and the tender maidens don't love
military men anymore, don't care for boots and shoulder marks
we're peace-loving people and only politicians and oligarchs
would still go to a shooting range when they got drunk

at times a mafia hitman would lay in wait for his prey
to come out jogging, shadowed by his bodyguards
also, the local bullies and racketeers who stalked like bulls
and world war two veterans occupied with community work

a german shepherd runs peacefully along the fence
lagging behind its owner, who holds a leash
war peers from the computer screen, it mouths
its trite lines, like: life's a game, people are pawns

*Translated from the Russian by Ostap Kin
and Polina Barskova*

* * *

when wars are over we just collapse
how do we restore the ruins what to do with the traps
the trenches and useful bunkers and ramparts
where did the damn enemy go the one we dragged
across europe and chased out with our raw force
and where in the world is our victory flag

all full of bullet and shrapnel holes but still victorious
where are the iron sword and the shield of brass
the chainmail and leather quiver filled with arrows
what will we do without all these objects
without our warrior ancestors and Lenin's words
and his commandments and soaring iron birds

when wars are over you don't know what to do anymore
it might even be nice if the enemy knocked on the door
killed your old mother raped your daughter or sister
then we can tighten our belts and stand shoulder to shoulder
march through europe and capture a capital city
and mark this tremendous day in the state calendar

Translated from the Russian by Olga Livshin
and Andrew Janco

* * *

modern warfare is too large for the streets —
a problem solved by a thousand-pound bomb
its contemporary weight equivalent is sixteen tons
as they sang in the fifties: *goodbye pretty girls*
goodbye company store
we're peaceful people our armored train stuffed with the spoils of war

we're peaceful people who happen to wear camouflage
three jolly fellows, the combat vehicle crew
broken-off pieces, an industrial collage
I still love my rifle, but a Kalashnikov is a must
the launch of a beautiful friendship in the rocket launcher
hot bullet, hot heart — only the sky is the limit

my beloved rifle, we've reached the end of our shining path
the streets tighten up, you dive into an alley
with all of your battle-ready equipment, your army, your navy
with all of your heart, it doesn't matter that's not the point
he's all muscle, ordinary-looking, possibly an idiot
firemen and militia are looking for him, he's the real hero

safety skills — some twist of the wrist, mind's of no use
stuff a cigarette with gunpowder and the empire goes up in smoke
you cross the boundary, no more boundaries as far as the eye can see
the sky's cloth is tattered and turns into a curtain fringe
black sun rises, a medal on God's chest
now, don't be sad — your life is behind you

Translated from the Russian by Ostap Kin
and Polina Barskova

* * *

My brother brought war to our crippled home.
War, a little girl, hair tied in bow — *she can barely walk on her own,*
my brother says, *she can stay with you, we'll go out, we'll hit the road,*
she's so little, she can't keep up, can't roam around alone!

My brother left, but war stayed, and she really is small.
She tried to help around the house, she swept the floor and all,
but she is sort of weird, she pokes around in the corner,
takes junk out of grandma's oak chests in no particular order.

At night she's restless — and we have no peace.
She keeps silent — we've had no days worse than these.
The windows are broken. It is too cold to stir.
And my brother still hasn't come back for her . . .

Translated from the Russian by Olga Livshin
and Andrew Janco

BESSARABIA, GALICIA, 1913–1939
PRONOUNCEMENTS

1
And rabbi Yitzchak Levi said:

"People and trees share this —
roots in the earth."

2
And rabbi Shraga Mendlowitz said:

"This observation is inexact
for the roots of trees are whole and quenched, even as the earth is dry,
while our roots —
our roots
are withered and torn."

3
And rabbi Yitzchak Steinmacher said:

"This difference is nonessential
for, whether living or dead: all roots still nurture."

4
And rabbi Shlomo ben Yehuda said:

"It's not up to us to say whether our roots are alive:
for we have a Helper,
who promised us eternal life —
and is true to his promise."

5
And rabbi Yitzchak Steinmacher said:

"Listening to you
I cannot help but think of a genealogical tree. We picture its trunk
                                                            ascending,

its branches —
mighty and wide; the name of our ancestor is a fruit
that's ripe.
In truth: a genealogical tree
descends
into the earth. Verily, not only its roots are in the earth
but so are its trunk
and branches.
As for us: we are the ignorant leaves
under the sun of Torah,
ignorant,
what do we say to each other?"

6
And rabbi Shraga Mendlowitz said:

"Ah!
It grieves me to think of a tree
that grows into its death,
that descends into the earth.
There might be a subtle deception
in this image:
for our roots are in the Earth,
while this earth is not the Earth,
but a desert of wandering. "

And raising his voice,
rabbi Shraga went on:
"Verily I say unto Thou:
if somebody dares
to sift in the finest of sieves through the sand of Sinai
in order to find the remains
of those traveling from Egypt, he'd find nothing,

for our roots are in the Earth,
and this earth — is not the Earth."

7
And all four of them said:

"Blessed be the tree growing into the Earth,
submerged into the Earth.
Blessed be You, Who
has this tree shaking
in awe,
shuddering end to end, from its thinnest twig to its root.
For this shudder,
for the chance
to know terror and to shudder from fear and pain,
is exactly
the proof of life."

Much later, in the 70ies,
after the Six-Day War,
archeologists attempted an excavation
in the Sinai desert
in search of what they call
material evidence of forty years of wandering
in the desert.

And they found? Nothing.

Translated from the Russian by Valzhyna Mort

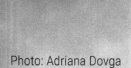

Photo: Adriana Dovga

MARIANNA KIYANOVSKA

* * *

I believed before
that Death turns sea to stone
Death is when the tide of the Earth covers us up

now I believe
Death is the Word
unknown to my soul

speak, Death
the unspeakable to my soul
what is death
tell me and return

enter my body
where my soul drifts
like a boat

this is what I will think about
again and from the very beginning

my Dear
your boat is in me

*Translated from the Ukrainian by Oksana Lutsyshyna
and Kevin Vaughn*

* * *

in a tent like in a nest
twilight, pleasant and still
smells of rosin
angel feathers, home
the nature of things reveals itself without warning
hands and throat ache from smoke
sweet and salty as blood
a flash fire breaches
the fabric beneath the skin
insomniacs trying to breathe
with shrinking lungs

tomorrow's light will freeze
somebody's
pupils and lips

and today it is time to gather the stones
dead and alive
warming them through body

teaching them to fly

*Translated from the Ukrainian by Oksana Lutsyshyna
and Kevin Vaughn*

* * *

we swallowed an air like earth
the kind of black
neighbors gardened together

and in that black
as in a fleshy cherry
sweet and bitter
and in that sweet and that bitter
salt and flesh

we stored in our lungs many years beforehand
not the cherry plum
another tree
some of us exhaled cherry pits
some bullets

stones bulged from their sockets
and became eyes

everything else became memory
air, fire

Translated from the Ukrainian by
Oksana Lutsyshyna and Kevin Vaughn

* * *

I wake up, sigh, and head off to war,
For the lilacs have already faded.
I scrub, I slice the skin off my palm
And feed death from my hand.
But death is not hungry, a fledgling
— a cuckoo chick — begs my pardon.
Don't go, she pleads,
There's nothing there.
I too have a soul, she says.
The lilacs have faded,
The orchards will bloom,
The war will come to an end.

Translated from the Ukrainian by Oksana Maksymchuk,
Max Rosochinsky, and Kevin Vaughn

* * *

The eye, a bulb, that maps its own bed,
Summons memory — not yet alive, but
Begun. Even the first war of my lifetime —
Doesn't mean death — just smoke.
A white skeleton, a holiday cup of water —
Emptied, crushed, carried out of the room.
Thistles whisper: get up and move.
A bullet wants to kiss you.

Translated from the Ukrainian by Oksana Maksymchuk,
Max Rosochinsky, and Kevin Vaughn

* * *

Their tissue is coarse, like veins in a petal,
They return from paradise seized, smoke
Hidden in the branched crown of irises. Blue —
Brown means that the eyeball's gone cloudy.
The cloud is mixed up: should it fly, walk or crawl,
And the cloud reads letters from home —
And the cloud breathes hard, rips its tissue
To shreds — living this way right up to death.

*Translated from the Ukrainian by Oksana Maksymchuk,
Max Rosochinsky, and Kevin Vaughn*

* * *

Things swell closed. It's delicious to feel how fully
The fruit ripens in your throat—such deadly vitality.
Warm to the touch, settled in the lungs' depth,
A silhouette, disembodied, fleshless.
First, it grows—like the fish that got away,
Then, it thickens, an eye slicing through glass.
The throat's on a line. The dusk thickens.
A cello bow draws the throat shut.

Translated from the Ukrainian by Oksana Maksymchuk,
Max Rosochinsky, and Kevin Vaughn

* * *

Naked agony begets a poison of poisons,
Matter repressed kisses the shell.
Beyond that, here's dirt underneath the fingernails.
Dregs discarded from the sieve. Speak of the wound:
how sand contains and releases the tide.
In musty trenches — the day's un-death — for only a moment.
God is born, comes of age, slumbers and is risen
Somewhere in a meadow near Luhansk,
Amongst the blood and hazel trees.

Translated from the Ukrainian by Oksana Maksymchuk,
Max Rosochinsky, and Kevin Vaughn

Photo: Oleksandr Laskin

HALYNA
KRUK

A WOMAN NAMED HOPE

it rained for four straight months
knocking down crops, trampling gardens
they came as new recruits
diligently watering the roadside bushes
as long as they could to slow their march to foreign war

and none of us knew
                                    where the war zone actually was
no one understood the true scope of the losses
when a woman called Hope came to lift our spirits
she had no intention of dying

each person, she told us, carries their own war
and a weapon
                    they'll clutch to the end,
and victory is a whore — she doesn't care where she lies
she belongs to anyone

and we listened to a roll of thunder leave her throat
while she sang to us strange marching drills and lullabies
every drop of her saliva a balm
containing the poison of love

because every woman, she warned, knows this kind of love
that brings her low, shoves a gun barrel in her mouth
and does not kill her. After, the rains pass through her,
                            troop after troop
washes away the blood.

Translated from the Ukrainian by Sibelan Forrester and
Mary Kalyna with Bohdan Pechenyak

* * *

like a blood clot, something
catches him in the rye
                      though in life
what is fair?
so he is annoying with his limping
through the hospital courtyard missing
a limb, as if he'd been limbless
in those unmiraculous fields,
so saturated with blood, no foot can fall
without grasping its own absence,
entered into war's tedious register
where limbs, faces, bodies are rejected
like blood from mismatched donors —
his unit's all scattered throughout the rye fields —
he begins to gather them up when he closes his eyes . . .
the women bring food, clothes, medicine
and, as is their habit, sit at his feet

Translated from the Ukrainian by Sibelan Forrester and
Mary Kalyna with Bohdan Pechenyak

* * *

someone stands between you and death — but
who knows how much more my heart can stand —
where you are, it's so important
someone prays for you
even with their own words
even if they don't clasp their hands and kneel

plucking the stems off strawberries from the garden
I recall how I scolded you when you were small
for squashing the berries before they ripened

my heart whispers: Death, he hasn't ripened yet
he's still green, nothing in his life has been
sweeter than unwashed strawberries
I beg you: oh God, don't place him at the front,
please don't rain rockets down on him, oh God,
I don't even know what a rocket looks like,
my son, I can't picture the war even to myself

Translated from the Ukrainian by Sibelan Forrester

* * *

like a bullet, the Lord saves those who save themselves,
like the bullet that the man in a trench
saves for his own temple

beyond the boundary that separates us from them
the harvest birds chirp to you that already
your son is kicking in the womb

hide yourself in a fir tree's needle, in a tiny boy's
face that falls through the junipers
to search for you

in a field that lies fallow, in the living soil,
you left for him the heaviest words:
"Fatherland" and "dad"

a Fatherland, passed from father to son,
replacing his father — one so young —
anyone would weep

"but God, let him feel, in his bones
that he is my last, truest bullet,
save him for me, oh Lord . . ."

Translated from the Ukrainian by Sibelan Forrester
and Mary Kalyna with Bohdan Pechenyak

Photo: Valentyn Kuzan

OKSANA LUTSYSHYNA

* * *

eastern europe is a pit of death and decaying plums
I hide from it in the body of america
but sooner or later I'll slip from this light
back down into that other
and will start talking about death because that is our national sport
talking about death
sad yet beautiful
hoping that the world will hear us and gasp at the beauty and sadness

my lover spreads my fingers with his own
he was educated in good old france
then america
he also studied buddhism and erotica somewhere near the borders
of thailand
it's good to drink wine with him and chat
but not about death or eastern europe
because the world's a shithole and it's worthwhile to learn only one art:
that of hopping from one pleasure islet to another
and not giving a damn about plague-infected continents with their
corpse-eating flies

he kisses me goodnight and disappears into his dream
as I lie in mine, full of summer sun and ephemeral sweetness
mitteleuropa zbigniew herbert whispers in my ear
middle europe enters a labyrinth without a single turn
a labyrinth of fate and freshly laid brick
it enters and doesn't exit

it endures and revives, small like newly seeded grass in the evening
strong like the grandchildren of those that survived the war
when, when will I die? — someone asks in my still childish voice
but I don't hear the answer because it suddenly becomes dark
in this death pit, where miklos radnoti is writing his last poem

*Translated from the Ukrainian by Oksana
Lutsyshyna and Olena Jennings*

* * *

don't touch live flesh
if you must, touch a wound no longer open
this one — let me embrace it
coil myself around it

leave it alone, let me carry it back home
alive in a boat of flesh
this resolute flower of summer
this most succulent of its berries

*Translated from the Ukrainian by
Oksana Maksymchuk and Max Rosochinsky*

* * *

he asks, don't help me
help the soldiers
I don't need anything anymore
neither medicine, nor heat, nor light
nor a drink of water

the room I'm leaving is not this one
but the room of my body
they say that God doesn't exist
that the One that exists is human
but as a human — can he exist?
is his existence necessary?

they say that I'm at the end of life
but I still don't understand anything

last night it hurt so bad
that I forgot everything, even who I was
no heaven, no blessed darkness
all I saw were soldiers
I felt their thirst in my bones

don't come to help me
help those who still want to

make children

*Translated from the Ukrainian by Oksana Maksymchuk
and Max Rosochinsky*

I DREAM OF EXPLOSIONS

someone sets a lighter to a bush of living fire
invisible
with an invisible hand

there's no place on earth that's safe
there's no earth anymore
there's nothing
how can we begin with the words:
"Nothing exists"?

the whole body becomes an organ of sight
finds a foothold
for true vision
you fall out of the world as out of a sieve
and you see: it's not there,
it's an illusion

so why does it still hurt
so bad

*Translated from the Ukrainian by Oksana Maksymchuk
and Max Rosochinsky*

Photo: Milena Androshchuk

VASYL
MAKHNO

FEBRUARY ELEGY

today the muse is the nurse
who is shot through the neck
in Maidan's winter winds
in the war now upon us
for which we are given wings

the student who now lies murdered
wrapped up in heavenly blankets
muse, please give us some advice
and hold tight onto the forceps
for the hour of death is nigh

in hearts that are shot right through
in ripped open stomachs and lungs
my muse, you, too, are bruised
an angel of death holding nails
while recording the names of the slain

who drags all the wounded aside
who strikes matches until they blaze
I see how he keeps up the fight
ripping asunder his greatcoat —
two-hundred-year-old Shevchenko

Translated from the Ukrainian by Uilleam Blacker

WAR GENERATION

each generation must fight its own war
each in that generation bears his own guilt
you may live in New York but you are always
a soldier of your unit — your country — its troubles

you're a soldier of the air — its commando
your country's army is a flying garden
shielding the heavens, the source that feeds
the earth beneath your feet, its simple seed

your sole defense is your heart — and a flak jacket
today you must forget that you are a poet
you must come here and stand — there's room in the ranks
merge into the Dnipro — its protective banks

your standard issue boots squeeze your feet
your unit digs trenches — and digs in its heels
each one's a soldier in this earth-seed generation
each one is capable of carrying a machine gun

war will come for each generation
filled up with light — but still more with scum
with the dirty boots of funeral guards
with mourning marches and army ballads

Translated from the Ukrainian by Uilleam Blacker

ON WAR

a soldier — he can catch a bullet
with his quivering heart and fall into solitude itself
the earth — like a mother — will embrace him
because an idiot sniper shot him
an angel lights a candle and sounds his trumpet

a battalion that no longer exists —
they were shot in the back at close range —
they're still tying their bootlaces
still marching through the steppe
already hopelessly late

the general — commander of a non-existent front
a turncoat swine and no hero —
deserves to have his epaulettes stripped
should grovel at every door
forget his hemorrhoids and heal his soul

this is war: mother and stepmother —
cousin, aunt and, sure, a whore,
death, lacking any semantic sense
when it gathers up its metal bowls
is a hole-riddled soldier's heart, nothing more

I am a poet of the periodic table of ruins
of a broken army and a forfeited land
shot-through like the heart of a soldier
it shakes like an uncatchable feather
trembling lightly on a stem

Translated from the Ukrainian by Uilleam Blacker

ON APOLLINAIRE

while we may call snow a flute — which among all the flutes
of language is the finest stem — the deepest well to hide
sounds, the fanfares of interwar silence, so beloved of the lieu-
tenant: who tells his soldiers to study the military trade

snow in the business of war is no fault of flutes or fanfares
a plane flies like an angel through the heavens, scattering the feathers
of the hawk's victim wrapped in white, like a cut-out sheet of darkness
nervously sealing the holes in the flute's ragged corpse

perhaps in that music between silver and bronze — all snow and water —
it rises like a sail, like a ship's pitch-covered bottom —
the lieutenant forgets orders and hallucinates: the almonds will flower
and the soldiers melt like snow through the village, seeking port wine

lucid in his dreams, he bleeds from his head — Apollinaire
has forgotten something — in the end he'll ask for pickled cabbage juice,
but there are no villagers here, the angel of death arrives, opens the door
shuts his eyes, wraps him in music, and then cuts loose

his boat on the river, the soldiers bring wine, sit downcast on the hilltop,
make a tent from their rifles and pull dried bread from their pockets
washing it down with their wine, sadness and surrealism —
death is here — all around them lurk ravens and foxes

Translated from the Ukrainian by Uilleam Blacker

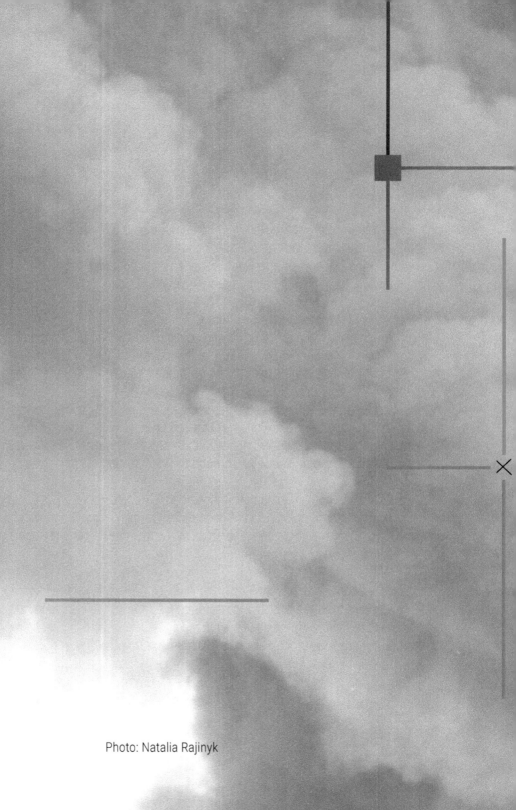

Photo: Natalia Rajinyk

MARJANA
SAVKA

* * *

We wrote poems
about love and war,
so long ago
we could have gone grey three times over—
in the days before we had war,
it seemed love would never burn out
and pain was in the offing
Yes, there *were* wounds there,
not just cracks in a chocolate heart,
but they managed to heal
and we went on living.
It wasn't mocking,
or some deliberate game.
We read the signs
on palimpsests of old posters,
on the walls of blackened buildings,
in coffee grounds.
What changed, my sister?
Our hot-air balloon
turned into a lead ball.
The metaphor — died.

Translated from the Ukrainian by Sibelan Forrester and
Mary Kalyna with Bohdan Pechenyak

* * *

Forgive me, darling, I'm not a fighter.
Every time you gaze into my face,
I tell you:
I have a knife to cut willow twigs —
I can weave you a basket —
If you like, I can weave you a bird,
And plant violets in its eyes.
I'm not a fighter, darling,
I have a knife to prune branches
On the young trees.
You haven't come out to the garden for so long.
The cherries are coming in.
Darling, why have you gone so grey?

Translated from the Ukrainian by Sibelan Forrester and
Mary Kalyna with Bohdan Pechenyak

* * *

january pulled him apart
february knocked him off his feet
spitting blood into the snow
he waited for his march —
but didn't know what shore
he'd be able to cling to
god, what a calendar —
blow after blow
his heart scarred
by such weird months:
Deathcember, Sorrowtober, or Bittertember
where even the trees grow
upside down, crowns up into roots
so young he barely lived
yet dying his death fully
then one day
the war died with him
and he was born again in may
amidst the grasses
or maybe he didn't really die
but just lay in the grass
under a wide open sky
under the sky everyone's alive

Translated from the Ukrainian by Sibelan Forrester and
Mary Kalyna with Bohdan Pechenyak

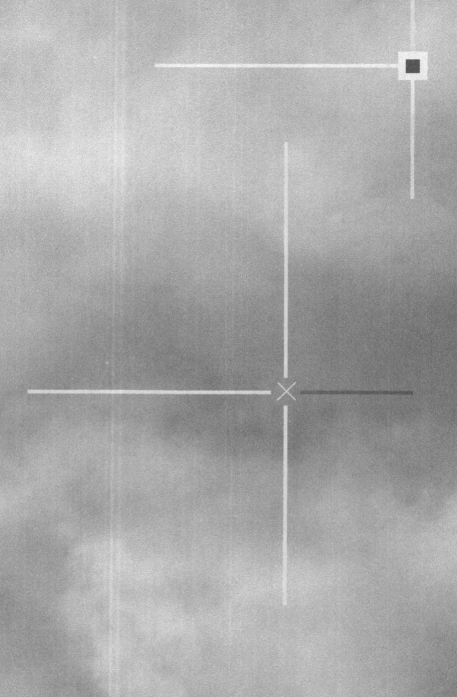

Photo: Oleksandr Laskin

OSTAP
SLYVYNSKY

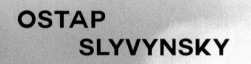

LOVERS ON A BICYCLE

She rides sitting on the frame, like a bird
perched on a branch, puffed-up, mature,
with two clenched
knees that signal sweetly
to the truck drivers passing by.

Him we don't see clearly, but we hear
his flask clanking against the seat with every
pedal stroke. He's humming a ditty,
where did he pick it up, which war zone? No one's heard it here.

She holds a handful of hazelnuts and feeds him
without turning — she passes them back and he
catches them with his mouth, which resembles
a fringed brown patch.

On the way back from the station she'll be alone,
looking like a paper doll,
dry, straight, two-dimensional,
used to making do with this love, as she
is used to making a meal out of nothing —
a dash of tea, a couple of potatoes.
She will ride through the first bout of rain,
reeling with her feet the over-exposed film — an endless
blank frame, where he runs into the living room
and spins her in his arms.

So it goes, this empty language of love, bargaining with hope,
like a one-legged chair with a stove: let me be
at least until midday. I won't
live through the night.

Translated from the Ukrainian by Anton Tenser
and Tatiana Filimonova

LIEUTENANT

I turned abruptly and drove down into the forest. Couldn't
take the road — another convoy was right behind us.
Bang! — and the fire receded, only to enfold us again the next moment.
Maybe someone decided to read us
through the tarpaulin envelopes,
illuminating every tiniest vein?

Those who believe in the balance of things can consider me justly
punished. A deserter? A man burnt to a cinder
embarrassed of showing himself to a doctor,
of having sex with lights on — and more than once.
A veteran laughingstock. A dopey uncle
for the kids in the family, who lets himself get drunk,
who accompanies the little ones, when they're kicked out
to play outside. Alone, with a future stuffed up with
colorful rags and a tattered blanket.

An example to no one. I spin in a chair, as if possessed
by a spirit: to the window — it's day, to the wall — it's night,
perfectly round, with a hole in the middle.

Translated from the Ukrainian by Anton Tenser
and Tatiana Filimonova

ALINA

She danced, since evenings were still warm,
and the world was being rolled up like
a carpet after a city festival,
and lights sparkled above red leaves.
She danced, because she wanted to turn back and
she knew you couldn't resurrect things by imagining them.
She danced, because it's better to remember with the body:
how she woke up, fell asleep
on the wet deck, waited for
things to be loaded. How she ran
after a floppy-eared dog, not wanting
to leave it to them.
She danced, because there are no more
places, stamps, return
addresses, banks, municipal headquarters, no more
street, water pump, half-painted
fence, soap dishes, brushes.
Everything is in a single moving point,
so compressed,
as a wrist where all the blood
has gathered.

*Translated from the Ukrainian by Anton Tenser
and Tatiana Filimonova*

1918

Sometimes even an exploding bullet
leaves only a tiny mark.
Likewise, all I remember from that war is
how one day, towards the end,
a horse
fell off a platform
when a train took a turn
and there was no one
to come back for him, no one
to pick him up from below the embankment,
kids gave him grass,
and he lay there
with broken legs and a dull eye,
charcoal black,
like a sign left by the retreating
night to mark a path for the night
that was to come.

Translated from the Ukrainian by Anton Tenser
and Tatiana Filimonova

KICKING THE BALL IN THE DARK

Toward whose goal were we kicking the ball in the dark,
when we could no longer tell treetops apart
from distant mountain ridges?
Zoran says to go back, there's a droning river ahead. Just beavers
with their murky treasures, that's all, the remains of old
swimming holes. Burning sheets fend off
the shadows when, exhausted, we think only of bed and firewood.
Solar plexus lit the chambers of the forest, a padlocked,
forsaken resort, fear, all the signs we could read,
we sensed the music and wanted to dance. Scattered
tin instruments of some sort were playing before our eyes.
"No one here talks to me anymore. They speak of the caliphate."
 A shattered brickyard, above it glows a sextant and the twinkling
hounds run loose. Zoran and Zorana in a gingerbread house, further up
a water boundary, somebody slept at the abandoned checkpoint,
                                        somebody saw
the children. An ill-fated longitude, by all accounts.
Light up the sextant, summon the angels, make them a bed in the
                                        brickyard,
I say to Zoran. Eagle folk, whom the Greeks
tell to take it in the mouth at the border crossing: I can feel
the blood turning heavily in the temples. "Dirty boots" and used horses,
children born on the road, the specially invited musicians,
sacks, in which flour turns to sand overnight,
and wine, which cannot turn back. Is it all invented by the blue eye,
                                        flickering
in the top right-hand corner? Does radio static speak to
us in the language of the spirits? Hate does not let you sleep
                            and drives you
to the mountain ridge in the middle of the night, tells you to shoot at
                                        the gaping sky.

Where's the office to file a complaint against fear?
Scraps of brass pipes resound in the branches of a tree, now
                                        entirely bare.
Autumn arrives here like an envelope with a tuft of grass, which
                                        ignites, burns,
doesn't go out, and dances in the dark like a fiery lung, and plays
                                        with the dark
some baffling game.

Translated from the Ukrainian by Anton Tenser
and Tatiana Filimonova

STORY (2)

She is warm, but inseparable from the freezing night,
like a handle from a knife.
                    Body —
that's her fragile embassy.
But her homeland is the dark alley,
where an outsider could get killed.
                    I know this,
I let half of her face live in darkness,
not moving the lamp.
And I don't ask,
        she offers her story.
Her kid wakes up,
skipping a beat of his sleep
                "Four days, —
she says. — That was the longest
we didn't come up.
On the third day — or was it night — we ran out of candles,
and I started recalling
            willfully
nothing too specific,
just a room with a window. A day,
which never began
and never ended.
            A night, when you go to sleep
and turn off the lights, knowing that in the darkness
trees blossom and nighttime birds hunt.
A morning,
        when you doze off on your feet and the oatmeal
just won't come to a boil.
                And perhaps all those years

of dull awakenings, when nothing happens,
are given to us
           so that we,
like a rock
that sits in the sun absorbing heat,
one awful night
           could warm somebody's cheek?"

Translated from the Ukrainian by Anton Tenser
and Tatiana Filimonova

LATIFA

The kid asks, of course . . . He asks
when we will head back home.
And so one time I told him. I said: our house
was taken up to the sky. I don't know
what I was thinking. I said:
our house was so good to us, Alim,
that it could not stand on earth anymore
like all other houses.
And it had so much love,
so many layers of love
we applied to the floor, the doors,
the window panes,
and as soon as the old love peeled off,
we would put on a new layer, even more diligently
and generously; ever brighter white and red
was the love we put on. Also, ivory-colored
love, although grandpa said that's not real love,
just childish games. Because for love
a simple color should be enough.
All of this I say to myself, and to the kid
I say: yes, you could see nothing but
the sky from the windows now.
And angels too.
But there is no one home.
Because angels are not for the living to see.

Translated from the Ukrainian by Anton Tenser
and Tatiana Filimonova

A SCENE FROM 2014

"For years I would wake up
when he returned from his night shift, around three or four
in the morning. He showered for a long time
and went to bed just as black, coal-like,
almost invisible
in the dark. Did he simply dissolve one night?"
                    We're silent.
In a moment she bursts into laughter: some kid
runs past us, trips
and falls — right on top of the flour sack that
he's carrying,
                    and his sneakers fly up high
in the heart of a little white cloud —
                            so white, this explosion,
she says, so quiet.

Translated from the Ukrainian by Anton Tenser
and Tatiana Filimonova

ORPHEUS

        But really this whole story
has a backstory, and it is about
a kid who was afraid of water.
But he would still go with everyone to the beach and clamber up
the long rock,
and when the boys jumped into the sea, he stayed behind,
standing there, skinny and lost,
        and watched them grow distant,
their heads in ruffles of splashes,
with the single hope —
that none of them look back.
And then he would head for the nearby
buildings, slashing thistle heads, helpless,
        different from everyone else here —
resembling a copper string, accidentally
weaved into a basket.
        You know this kid?
You know at what point
music comes out of anger, like a butterfly
emerging out of a frostbitten cocoon?
You know where he was until morning, when
his parents found him in the grass, sweaty,
        with clenched teeth?
And tell me this: how much anger can a poem hold?
Just enough to
drown out the sirens?

Translated from the Ukrainian by Anton Tenser
and Tatiana Filimonova

Photo: Nata Koval

LYUBA
YAKIMCHUK

DIED OF OLD AGE

granddad and granny passed away
they died on the same day
at the same hour
at the same moment —
people said, they died of old age

their hen met its end
and so did their goat and their dog
(their cat was out)
and people said, they died of old age

their cottage fell apart
their shed turned into ruins
and the cellar got covered with dirt
people said, everything collapsed from old age

their children came to bury the granddad and granny
Olha was pregnant
Serhiy was drunk
and Sonya was only three
they all perished, too
and people said, they died of old age

the cold wind plucked yellow leaves and buried beneath them
the granddad, the granny, Olha, Serhiy and Sonya
who all died of old age

Translated from the Ukrainian by Anatoly Kudryavitsky

HOW I KILLED

I remain connected to my family over the phone
with all of my family connections wiretapped
they are curious: whom do I love more, mom or dad?
what makes my grandma cry out into the receiver?
intrigued as ever by my sister's war-fueled drama with her boyfriend
who used to be my boyfriend

all of my phone connections are blood relations
my blood is wiretapped
they must know what percentage is Ukrainian
Polish, Russian, and if there's any Gypsy
they must know how much of it I gave, and to whom
they must know whether that's my blood sugar dropping
or the roof collapsing over me
and whether it's possible to build borders out of membranes

hundreds of graves have been dug between me and my mother
and I don't know how to leap over them
hundreds of mortar shells fly between me and my father
and I can't see them as birds
the metal doors of a basement, secured with a shovel
separate me from my sister
a screen of prayers hangs between me and my grandmother
thin silky walls muting out the noise, and I hear nothing

it's so simple, to stay connected over the phone
to add minutes to my calling cards, restless nights, Xanax
it must feel so intoxicating
to listen to someone else's blood throbbing in your earphones
as my blood clots into a bullet:
BANG!
!

Translated from the Ukrainian by Oksana Maksymchuk
and Max Rosochinsky

CATERPILLAR

her digits contract in the cold
a wedding band slips off her ring finger
it clinks and rolls on the pavement
her hands tremble like leaves
as a caterpillar draws near —
its track
crawls by her daughter's feet
and stops

two men approach
order her to open her hands
as if to clap
they peer into her passport, pass it between themselves
they press and squeeze her thumbs
on her index finger
they locate a burn instead of a callus
from shooting a sniper rifle
they call her by her nickname
or maybe it's someone else's —
Butch

they strip her
they probe her
they lay her down
as a queue
nine of them
(her favorite number)
rape her
wearing blue bathrobes
(her favorite color)

second-hand Nikes
(her favorite shoes)
nine of them
on one disheveled —
not bitch, but
woman
her little girl curls up like a fetus
looks on without tears
she picks up her mom's wedding band
holds it in her mouth
like a dog with a bone
and watches a caterpillar devour
their green town

Translated from the Ukrainian by Oksana Maksymchuk
and Max Rosochinsky

DECOMPOSITION

nothing changes on the eastern front
well, I've had it up to here
at the moment of death, metal gets hot
and people get cold

don't talk to me about Luhansk
it's long since turned into *hansk*
Lu had been razed to the ground
to the crimson pavement

my friends are hostages
and I can't reach them, I can't *do netsk*
to pull them out of the basements
from under the rubble

yet here you are, writing poems
ideally slick poems
high-minded gilded poems
beautiful as embroidery

there's no poetry about war
just decomposition
only letters remain
and they all make a single sound — rrr

Pervomaisk has been split into *pervo* and *maisk*
into particles in primeval flux
war is over once again
yet peace has not come

and where's my *deb, alts, evo*?
no poet will be born there again
no human being

I stare into the horizon
it has narrowed into a triangle
sunflowers dip their heads in the field
black and dried out, like me
I have gotten so very old
no longer Lyuba
just a *-ba*

*Translated from the Ukrainian by Oksana Maksymchuk
and Max Rosochinsky*

HE SAYS EVERYTHING WILL BE FINE

he says: they bombed your old school
he says: food supplies are running out and there's no money left
he says: the white lorries with humanitarian aid are our only hope
he says: shells from the white lorries just flew overhead

there's no school any more
how can it be that there's no school?
is it empty? is it full of holes, or has it been totally destroyed?
what happened to my photo hanging on the roll of honour?
what happened to my teacher sitting in the classroom?

he says: photo? who gives a damn about your photo?
he says: the school has melted — this winter is too hot
he says: I haven't seen your teacher, please don't ask me to look for her
he says: I saw your godmother; she's no longer with us

run away you all
drop everything and run away
leave your house, your cellar with apricot jam jars
and pink chrysanthemums on the terrace
shoot your dogs, so they don't suffer
abandon this land, just go

he says: don't talk nonsense, we throw dirt on coffins daily
he says: everything will be fine, salvation will come soon
he says: the humanitarian aid is on the way

Translated from the Ukrainian by Anatoly Kudryavitsky

EYEBROWS

no-no, I won't put on a black dress
black shoes and a black shawl
I'll come to you all in white —
if I have a chance to come
And I'll be wearing nine white skirts
One beneath the other
I'll sit down in front of the mirror
(it'll be hung up with a cloth)
strike up a match
it'll burn out and I
will moisten it with my tongue
and draw black eyebrows
over my own, also black
then I'll have two pairs of eyebrows
mine and yours above them
no-no, I won't put on a black dress
I'll put on your black eyebrows
on me.

Translated from the Ukrainian by Svetlana Lavochkina

FUNERAL SERVICES

this terrorist looks like a bush
he trembles in the wind and sheds his leaves
but breath escapes from his mouth —
that's quite a disadvantage
for someone who wants to be a bush

this terrorist looks like snow
he is soft and white, but
warm skin is a disadvantage for someone
trying to look like snow

this terrorist looks like a pretty girl
she smiles at me
she hopes to entice me to kiss her
to seduce me into her terrorism
through carnal knowledge
she is also at a disadvantage:
I prefer boys

this terrorist is riding in a hearse
with a sign "mortuary services"
and it's true, his services are ghoulish
he himself doesn't enjoy the business

he lies in his coffin
pale as a corpse
cold as snow
breathless as a bush

he's so perfect
he has trained his heart to stop at will
at a checkpoint and accidentally
stopped it forever

he'd be so perfect
if you could only convince yourself that
he's just a terrorist, not a human being

Translated from the Ukrainian by Oksana Maksymchuk
and Max Rosochinsky

CROW, WHEELS

when the city was destroyed
they started fighting over the cemetery
it was right before Easter —
wooden crosses over the freshly dug graves
put out their paper blossoms —
red, blue, yellow,
neon green, orange, raspberry pink

joyful relatives poured vodka for themselves
and for the dead—straight onto their graves
and the dead asked for more, and more, and more
and their relatives kept pouring

the celebration carried on
but at some point
a young man tripped over the stretchers
at the grave of his mother-in-law,
an old man gazed into the sky
and lost it forever
a fat man smashed his shot glass
damaging the fence around his wife's grave
glass fell at his feet
like hail

Easter came
now a live crow sits on the grave
of Anna Andriivna Ravenova
instead of a headstone
BTR-80 wheels
rest at the cemetery nest of the Kolesnyk family

where lie buried
Maria Viktorivna, Pylyp Vasylyovych, and Mykola Pylypovych

what are they to me, those wheels and that crow?
I can no longer remember

*Translated from the Ukrainian by Oksana Maksymchuk
and Max Rosochinsky*

KNIFE

with relatives, we share table and graves
with enemies — only graves
one such candidate comes
to share a grave with me
says to me:
I'm bigger than you
I'm harder than you
I'm tougher than you
sticks knife after knife into my stomach and below
knife after knife
his pressure springlike
but

he is smaller than us
he is softer than us
because he's only got one knife
and there are plenty of us
at the table
and each has their own "but"
and each has their own cut

says to me I'm a sharper blade cut you
I'm a thicker blade cut you
chip, chop, chip, chop,
the last one is dead.
hold on they say hold on
and we hold onto our table

from the gun muzzle
we all drink our bullets
we pour our enemy one, too.

Translated from the Ukrainian by Svetlana Lavochkina

Photo: Valentyn Kuzan

**SERHIY
ZHADAN**

from STONES

We speak of the cities we lived in —
that went
into night like ships into the winter sea,

we speak of the cities that suddenly lost their ability to resist —
in front of our
eyes, like a circus show where every acrobat
dies, and so does each laughing clown; enchanted,
you watch,
never turning away (and inconspicuously
on the circus set
you grow up).

* * *

Now we remember: janitors and the night-sellers of bread,
gray, like wrapping paper,
burglars,
taxi drivers with klaxons instead of hearts,
children who grew up
among the old furniture
(furniture smelled of poplar trees and sea).

Our city of workers and ugly middle-men,
tearjerking market beggars
they cleared
the autumn fog
with their shouts.

We got to soak in the rain
with strangers
on tram stops,
old proletarian quirks, subway cars,
we got to soak in the rain
on cars
loaded with the unemployed
like magazines with cartridges
. . .

Translated from the Ukrainian by Valzhyna Mort

from WHY I AM NOT ON SOCIAL MEDIA

NEEDLE

Anton, age thirty-two.
Status: "living with parents."
Orthodox, but didn't go to church,
finished college, took English as his foreign language.
Worked as a tattoo artist, had a signature style,
if you can call it that.
Lots of folks from our local crowd passed through
his skillful hands and sharp needle.
When all this started, he talked a lot about
politics and history, started going to rallies,
fell out with friends.
Friends took offense, clients disappeared.
People got scared, didn't get it, left town.
You feel a person best when you touch her with a needle.
A needle stings, a needle stitches. Beneath
its metallic warmth the texture of a woman's skin is so supple,
the bright canvas of male skin's so stiff.
Piercing that outer shell,
you release the body's velvet beads
of blood. Carve, carve out
angels' wings on the submissive surface of the world.
Carve, carve, tattoo artist, for our calling
is to fill this world with meaning, to fill it
with colors. Carve, tattoo artist, this
outer lining, which hides souls and diseases —
all that we live for, all that we will die for.
Someone said they shot him at a roadblock,
in the morning, a weapon in his hands, somehow by accident —
No one knew what happened.

They buried him in a mass grave (they buried them all that way).
His possessions were returned to his parents.
Nobody updated his status.
There will come a time when some bastard
will surely write heroic poems about this.
There will come a time when some other bastard
will say this isn't worth writing about.

Translated from the Ukrainian by
Amelia Glaser and Yuliya Ilchuk

HEADPHONES

Sasha, a quiet alcoholic, esoteric, poet,
spent the whole summer in the city.
Surprised when the shelling started,
he turned on the news, then quit watching.
He roams the city, never removing his headphones,
listening to dinosaurs,
he runs into burnt out cars,
and dismembered bodies.

All of history,
the world where we once lived,
has left us the words and music of a few geniuses
who tried, and failed, to warn us,
tried to explain something or other,
but explained nothing, saved no one.
In graveyards,
their genius rib cages
sprout flowers and grass.
Nothing else will be left —
just the music, just the words, just a voice
forcing us to love.

You never have to turn this music off.
Listen to outer space, your eyes shut tight.
Think about whales in the night ocean.
There's nothing else to hear.
Nothing else to see.
Nothing else to feel.
Except the smell, of course.
Except the smell of corpses.

Translated from the Ukrainian by Amelia Glaser
and Yuliya Ilchuk

SECT

Andriy and Pavlo, Adventists, students,
daddy a businessman supported the community,
home — school — church was how they
lived their lives,
went there daily, lent a hand
whenever something needed fixing, shared pictures
on social media, gave shoutouts.
Even during those quiet years such devotion looked sectarian,
but once it all broke out — they were hunted
down. Some have moved, others were in hiding.
The two brothers were captured and shut in a basement.
They were ordered to bury the dead, to dig new graves.
They tried offering money, wept, grew paranoid.
They were moved to a different hole. Then they were forgotten
as if they never were.
In the black basement they sat listening to the dark,
early on they prayed, then quit praying —
ashamed of each other.
You lose faith when you are offered to die for it.
Who needs faith after they have seen the true ways of the world?
Why to believe in things that lost all meaning?
What about all those saints
with open stigmata on their bodies? What happened
to those stigmata? Did they close by themselves
like roses close at dusk? Or did they bleed,
infected, burning under the bandages?
Men with eyes blind from darkness
came to the hospital for wound dressing,
clenched their teeth when a nurse ripped off
old bandages, and young blood
sickled onto the dark skin. They asked

for painkillers, something, anything.
But there doesn't exist a pill for what
hurts them, it simply doesn't.

Translated from the Ukrainian by Valzhyna Mort

RHINOCEROS

Half a year she's held firm.
Half a year she's observed death
the way you observe a rhinoceros at the zoo —
dark folds,
heavy breathing.
She's scared, but doesn't look away,
doesn't close her eyes.

It's terrifying, really terrifying.
And it should be.
Death is terrifying, it frightens.
It's terrifying to smell the stink of a blood moon.
It's terrifying to see how history is made.

Half a year ago everything was completely different.
Half a year ago everyone was different.
No one got scared
when stars fell over the reservoir.
No one startled when smoke
rose from cracks in the black earth.

In the middle of the night street,
in the middle of the clamor and headlights,
in the middle of death and love
she buries her face in his shoulder,
pounds him desperately with her fists,
weeps, screams in the dark.
"I don't," she says, "want to see all this."
"I can't carry all this inside me.
"What do I need so much death for?
"What am I supposed to do with it?"

What can you do with death?
Carry it on your back,
like a Gypsy child —
Nobody loves him,
and he loves no one.
There is so little love,
love is so defenseless.

Cry and shatter the dark with your warm hands.
Cry and don't step away.
The world will never be the way it was before.
We'll never let it
be the way it was before.

Ever fewer lighted windows on the cold street.
Ever fewer carefree passers-by
around the shop windows.
In the hellish autumn dusk, fields and rivers cool.
The bonfires go out in the rain.
The cities grow numb at night.

Translated from the Ukrainian by Amelia Glaser
and Yuliya Ilchuk

THIRD YEAR INTO THE WAR

They buried him last winter.
Some winter too — not a snowflake, so much rain.
A quick funeral — we all have things to do.
Which side was he fighting for? I ask. What a question, they say,
One of the sides, who could figure them out.
What difference does it make, they say, same difference.
Only he could have answered, they say, now it's he said-she said.
Could he? His corpse is missing a head.

Third year into the war, bridges are patched.
I know so much about you — now what?
I know, for one, that you liked this song.
I know your sister, I loved her once.
I know your fears and where they came from.
I know who you met that winter and what was said.
Three years of nights patched with ash and star light.
I remember you always played for another school.
And yet, who did you fight for in this war?

To come here, every year, to rip dry grass.
To dig the earth, every year — dead, heavy earth.
To see, every year, this peace, this ill.
To tell yourself, till the end, that you didn't shoot
into your own. In the waves of rain — birds vanish.
I'd ask to pray for your sins, yet what sins?
I'd ask for the rains to stop — rains full of birds.
Some birds! It's easy for them. For all they know,
there's neither salvation nor soul.

Translated from the Ukrainian by Valzhyna Mort

THREE YEARS NOW WE'VE BEEN TALKING ABOUT THE WAR

+

A guy I know volunteered.
Returned six months later.
Where he was — I don't know.
What he's afraid of — he won't say.
But he's afraid of something.
It seems he's afraid
of everything.

He was normal enough before he left,
maybe talked a bit too much.
About everything on earth,
About every little thing he saw in front of him.

But when he returned he was
totally different, as if
someone had ripped out his old tongue
and forgot to replace it.

Now he spends all day in bed
listening to demons in his head.

The first demon is fierce,
a fire-spitter, demanding
punishment for all living beings.

The second demon is mild,
talks of forgiveness,
speaks softly,

puts his hands, smeared with black earth,
right on your heart.

The third demon's the worst.
He gets along with both.
Agrees with both, won't contradict.
Just his voice alone
gives you a migraine.

Translated from the Ukrainian by Virlana Tkacz and Bob Holman

++

Three years now we've been talking about the war.
We've learned how to talk about our own past in terms of the war.
We've learned to make our plans taking the war into account.

We have the words to express our anger.
We have the words to express our grief.
We have the words to express our contempt.
We have curse words, words for prayer,
we have all the necessary words
to talk about ourselves during the war.

It's very important for us to talk about ourselves during the war.
We cannot stop talking about ourselves during the war.
It's impossible to be quiet about ourselves.

Every morning we talk about the war.
We stand in front of the mirror, talk about the war.
We talk to the person we see.
Wise words.
Wise, convincing words.
Wise questions.
Wise answers.

Every morning we remind everyone about the number killed.
After lunch we savor flashes of sun light,
the living grass pushing through dead rock.
And in the evening we again remind everyone
about the number killed.

It is very important for us to remind everyone about the number killed.
It is very important that we remind everyone about the number killed.
It is very important that everyone hear about the number killed.

We don't give anyone else the chance.
We cut reality with garden shears,
evaluate it,
pronounce the diagnosis unfavorable.

For three years we've been evaluating.
For three years we've been talking to the mirror.
Where there's no chance of getting a difficult question,
there's no chance of getting an awkward reply

The more confident
talk about this out loud.
The less confident — quietly.

Either way, it doesn't influence
the number killed.

Translated from the Ukrainian by Virlana Tkacz and Bob Holman

+++

So that's what their family is like now.
So that's how their family talks now.
They have agreed not to argue,
to survive the summer
under fire.

So,
they don't talk about politics,
no arguing,
they don't talk about religion,
no arguing,
and they don't talk about god,
no arguing.

They don't talk about family members,
who left.
They don't talk about friends,
who stayed.
They don't talk about the guy from across the street,
who is at the front.

They do talk about the neighbor.
You can talk about the neighbor.
The neighbor died.
They feel sorry for the neighbor.

True, god also died.
But they don't feel sorry for him.
They don't feel sorry for him at all.

Translated from the Ukrainian by Virlana Tkacz and Bob Holman

++++

Sun, terrace, lots of green.
A boy and a girl,
probably students, sit at the table,
waiting for their order.
Near them on the table class notes,
piles of papers,
they probably dashed in here for lunch
between classes — and will run off soon.
So grown up, so serious.

What else?

They probably rent their apartment,
don't like to cook,
eat wherever.

They don't like to waste time in the kitchen.
They don't like to waste time on insignificant things.
Treat life like clothes,
try them on before you buy.
Learn not to waste time
on stupid things.

One day she will definitely have her own home.
One day he will definitely find a normal job.
It will be important to learn about everything,
to learn to select
the proper words to talk about love and humanity.
Dust, flowers, lots of green.
Last year's spring.

This is the only photo in which we're together — she says.
I was angry at him,
see, I'm looking away,
not speaking with him.
Then the war began.
He went off to war.
And that was that.

Translated from the Ukrainian by Virlana Tkacz and Bob Holman

+++++

The street. A woman zigzags the street.
A pause. By the grocery
she hesitates.
Shall she buy bread, there is not — is there enough? — not enough bread
at home.
Shall she buy bread now, or — tomorrow? — she considers.
Stares at. Stares at her phone. Rings. Rings.
Speaks to mother: Mother.
Speaks abruptly, without listening
she shouts.
Shouts
by the store window; at the store window,
as if she is shouting at herself in the store window.
Slaps the phone.
Zigzags the street, cursing
her invisible — and therefore even more
cursed — mother.

Tears. Tears of pain at her
mother
and at the impossibility of forgiving
her mother. Forget
the bread.
Forget it. Forget the bread and everything else on this earth. Forget it.
Forgo it. Leave it alone.

That morning
it begins. The first aerial bombardment.

Translated from the Ukrainian by Ilya Kaminsky

++++++

Village street —
gas line's broken.
Accident site. Danger.

Emergency crew isn't coming —
no one wants to be out during shootings.
When you call them — they're silent,
don't say anything,
like they don't understand you.

In the store next to the day-old bread,
they sell funeral wreaths.
There's no one out in the street —
everyone's left.

There are no lines.
Not for the bread,
not for the wreaths.

Translated from the Ukrainian by Virlana Tkacz and Bob Holman

+++++++

At least now, my friend says,
I know what the war is like.

Well, what's it like then? I ask him.

Like . . . Nothing, he answers.

He says it with confidence:
since he was captured, he can speak about most things
with confidence, through that experience.
In other words, with hate.

When he talks, better not to interrupt:
he won't let your words in, anyway.
He's got his position, and that's that,
He considers it the greatest honor
to hold one's position in times of war.
To deny the sun, to deny
the currents of the ocean.

So that's that:
the war is like . . . Nothing.
That is why we talk about it
without adjectives.

How did you feel?
Like . . . Nothing,
How did they treat you?

Like . . . Nothing.
How do you talk about all this?
Like . . . Nothing.
Now, how the hell do we live with all this?

Translated from the Ukrainian by Virlana Tkacz and Bob Holman

THIRTY-TWO DAYS WITHOUT ALCOHOL

A good day is a day
without bad news.
Sometimes everything turns out fine —
no news,
no fiction.

Three thousand steps to the supermarket
frozen chickens
like stars
gleam after death.
All you need
is mineral water,
I only need
my mineral water.
Managers,
like frozen chickens,
hatch the eggs
of profit
in the twilight.

Three thousand steps walking back home.
All I need is to hold on
to my mineral water,
to hold on
and keep count:
thirty-two days without alcohol
thirty-three days without alcohol
thirty-four days without alcohol.

Two birds perch on my shoulders,
and the one on the left keeps repeating:

thirty-two days without alcohol
thirty-three days without alcohol
thirty-four days without alcohol.

And the one on the right chimes in:
twenty-eight days till getting wasted
twenty-seven days till getting wasted
twenty-six days till getting wasted.

And the one on the left drinks the blood of Christ
from a silver chalice.
And the one on the right — the simpler one —
drinks some crap,
some diet coke.

On top of that
both of them are drinking
on my tab.

Translated from the Ukrainian by Ostap Kin

TAKE ONLY WHAT IS MOST IMPORTANT

Take only what is most important. Take the letters.
Take only what you can carry.
Take the icons and the embroidery, take the silver,
Take the wooden crucifix and the golden replicas.

Take some bread, the vegetables from the garden, then leave.
We will never return again.
We will never see our city again.
Take the letters, all of them, every last piece of bad news.

We will never see our corner store again.
We will never drink from that dry well again.
We will never see familiar faces again.
We are refugees. We'll run all night.

We will run past fields of sunflowers.
We will run from dogs, rest with cows.
We'll scoop up water with our bare hands,
sit waiting in camps, annoying the dragons of war.

You will not return and friends will never come back.
There will be no smoky kitchens, no usual jobs,
There will be no dreamy lights in sleepy towns,
no green valleys, no suburban wastelands.

The sun will be a smudge on the window of a cheap train,
rushing past cholera pits covered with lime.
There will be blood on women's heels,
tired guards on borderlands covered with snow,

a postman with empty bags shot down,
a priest with a hapless smile hung by his ribs,
the quiet of a cemetery, the noise of a command post,
and unedited lists of the dead,

so long that there won't be enough time
to check them for your own name.

Translated from the Ukrainian by Virlana Tkacz and Wanda Phipps

TRACES OF US

A city where she ended up hiding
a city on fire with flags, built under snowed-up passes,
hunters chase wild fowl out of protestant churches,
blue stars fall into a lake
killing slow-moving fish.
These streets where funambulists hover,
how they balance in school
windows, arousing joy,
how they dodge seagulls,
that snatch from her hands
weightless potato chips made of gold.
There, where we used to live together once,
we had no time for peace and meditation.
We slashed ourselves on the sharp cane of night,
dropped our clothes like ballast into the black elevator shaft
in order to hover in the air a little longer,
we hated, didn't forgive,
didn't accept, didn't trust,
and lived the best days
of our lives in anger.
But this city where she ended up hiding
gently touches her hand
and opens its warehouses and storages rooms.
These ports, the destination of the Senegalese
who arrive in cargo holds,
the black meat of their hearts,
the ivory bone of their eyes,
these cellars packed with cheese,
cheery protestant cities,
where one can wait through the Last Judgment,
for local lawyers are excellent

and walls unassailable.
Yet there, where the two of us used
to warm ourselves in the kitchens
by the blue sources of fire, there isn't a single
trace of us left. Time, an old funambulist,
fell down a hundred times and got back up a hundred times,
with broken collarbones and iron teeth,
time doesn't care which direction to run,
it licks the wounds, and returns to dancing with seagulls.
But the city where she managed to hide in —
how bright are its shirts and dresses,
how smooth the skin of pilots
and Chinese students.
And this fresh mountain air,
like the taste of lips after
exhausting kissing.
She forgot nothing in the place she left.
Not a single voice, not a single curse.
Life is a jolly tug of war
with angels on one side
and lawyers on the other.
Lawyers outnumber
but their services are more costly.

Translated from the Ukrainian by Valzhyna Mort

AFTERWORD

ON DECOMPOSITION AND ROTTEN PLUMS: LANGUAGE OF WAR IN CONTEMPORARY UKRAINIAN POETRY

Polina Barskova

When watching Sergey Loznitsa's astounding and difficult documentary "Maidan" (2014), one constantly faces a sense or even multiple senses of confusion: historical, spatial, and sonic. One wonders what is happening in the city of Kyiv. What is the perspective that camera offers to the audience, and what are all these strange sounds, where do they come from? One can discern fragments of popular folk songs and the national anthem, endlessly repeated "Glory to Ukraine! Glory to Heroes!", sounds of steps—and starting from the middle of the film, terrifying sounds of shooting and explosions . . .

And together in all of this "music of Revolution," to borrow from Alexander Blok's famous poem about the world of the revolutionary sensory perceptions, we hear poetry. In his complex soundtrack, Loznitsa includes the first sounds and words of poetry that were being born by that huge emotional impulse called the Revolution of Dignity. We perceive a disembodied voice pronouncing: "It's lies and slavery around / The humble folk forever silent / And on the throne of Ukraine / A greedy bandit keeps his reign."[1] Thus emerged the popular, yet naïve-sounding poetry of the barricades; it expressed the hopes and despair of a people ready for fatal change.

The impulse to create poetry out of the spirit of political uproar organizes this anthology. It shows us developments of the original urge—to speak the Revolution—by exploring growth and changes in Ukrainian poetry in the years after the upheaval of the 2014 Euromaidan and during the Russo-Ukrainian "hybrid-war" in Donbas. During these years, poetry writing in Ukraine acquired a new vitality, diversity, and strong national resonance—especially when it comes to political poetry.

I argue that Ukrainian literary identity is being shaped today within the realm of poetical expression. Following the idea of the Russian Formalist Yuri Tynianov on the significance of "smaller literary forms" for the dialogue between aesthetic and political discourses,[2] I suggest looking at the field of contemporary Ukrainian political poetry as a rhetorical laboratory where new forms of political expression and reaction are being worked out: and the present anthology gives us apt material for such exploration. What we see here is gradual development of certain tropes and devices, new kinds of collaboration between prose and poetry, new approaches to the task of representing experience of historical trauma: from the original impulse of Revolution, poetic language proceeds to the difficult and yet exhilarating work of mourning.

The *Words for War* anthology presents an extensive (even if not exhaustive) map of poetical utterances that emerged in Ukraine in reaction to political events: what I see as the anthology's strength is its diversity—many and different voices are introduced here, a volatile, melancholic, cacophonous chorus of attempts to speak what cannot be spoken: horror, fear, disgust. In my afterword, I am not able, for the shortage of allotted space, to cover the whole territory of this poetry, so I would like to talk about some poems and some poetries that strike me as offering radical discoveries within that centuries-long tradition of writing poetry about political upheavals and wars.

War and language, and war and poetry, became connected in the Western canon starting from—at least—the *Iliad* (which curiously is mentioned in the volume in a poem by Aleksandr Kabanov). Writing poetry about wars has been one of the medium's main jobs, unfortunately—mourning the dead and glorifying those who sent them to die. Each war brings its own knowledge, its own epiphany: thus the Great War of 1914–18, which resulted in the largest number of victims in human history, brought about the horror of a massive and "anonymous" destruction. The massacre left witnesses of this destruction (both in the military and among the civilians) without any hope of forgetting what happened to them—this trauma leading, among many other things, to the great literature of the "lost generation." Later in the twentieth century, Soviet history alone (Soviet Union being the empire that devoured and attempted to conflux Russia and Ukraine) engendered very powerful ways to write about the War and the Revolution. Though Soviet revolutionary and war poetry is a voluminous topic, I am happy to reduce it here to a short and brilliantly unbearable poem by a Ukraine-born Jew Ion Degen:

My friend in the throes of agony,
Don't call for your friends – it's in vain:
Let me warm the palms of my hands
In your blood that is getting cold.
Don't cry, don't whine like a cry-baby,
You're not wounded – you've been killed all right.
Let me instead take your felt boots off:
I have the whole war in front of me.

What makes the poetry in this anthology different from the previous waves and ways of war writing is, first, the subject matter—it describes a new kind of the military conflict—a so-called hybrid war—an undeclared murky political conflict without clear rules and borders, a war that touches everyone involved.

I speak here on several poetic strategies revealed by the anthology, covering poets of different generations and even different languages but who all write with an equal energy of indignation, abjection towards the war. If the task of the afterword is to arrive at some kind of conclusion, to summarize the newly occurred fact of literature that is represented by an anthology—then I am convinced that this anthology shows that the Ukrainian revolution and Russo-Ukrainian War has already led to the emergence of new poetics. Here are some of its major events.

The Case of Zhadan: Poetics of Witness

The literary works of Serhiy Zhadan, perhaps one of the most examined contemporary Ukrainian literary figures, underwent a significant change following the events in Maidan. As a resident of Kharkiv, which for the duration of the twentieth century was a hub for both Ukrainian and Russian poetry, Zhadan was equally interested in Ukrainian and Russian postmodernism and European modernism (Zhadan himself singles out the importance of Celan and Milosz). Zhadan underwent a development from neoromanticism, a style which focused mostly on his creative self, towards a considerably less traditional, *prosaic* poetics of evidence and inter-subjectivity. In his 2015 collection of poetry and translations, "Life of Maria" (in Ukrainian, *Zhyttia Marii*), Zhadan recreates various voices and narratives of the participants of the political crisis on both sides of the conflict, aiming to explore varieties of the political agendas or lack thereof. This desire to dissect the conflict beyond right and wrong with a much more complex and individualistic approach led to the radical change of his style—what he's been doing recently can be called *journalistic poetry.*

In his poetry about the Donbas war, Zhadan radically challenges our expectations as readers—this poetry strikes one as radically antipoetic: each of the texts in the cycle "Why I am Absent in the Social Media" presents a sketch-portrait (a traditionally popular form of war writing—but in prose) of an individual devastated and marginalized by the war. In its quasi-prosaic quality, Zhadan's war poetry nevertheless does not fail to call our attention—like shadows in a drawing—to the presence of those whom the war events are ready to count as absent even before their death. Following the figurations of influential philosopher Giorgio Agamben, Zhadan is preoccupied with the ethnography of the *bare life* of this war: lives of those abandoned by the state, dolefully existing at its meager margins.

This new form of acute linguistic attention is connected to Zhadan's work as a civil interlocutor—not only has he been reading to a variety of audiences all over Ukraine, but also he is known for actively voicing concerns about the Ukrainian population of Donbas and traveling there when possible.[3]

The Younger Generation: Reconstructions of Language Shattered by War

Poets of the younger generation who are significantly interested in the works of Zhadan follow him in a desire to connect poetics and politics and to extend their literary experimentations into different directions. One of the most linguistically daring figures of the younger generation is Lyuba Yakimchuk. She has been exploring the potential of broken or "bad" language, language that bears aphatic traces of war, that shows destruction. In her book *Apricots of Donbas* (2015), which, among other things, narrates Yakimchuk's and her family's forced escape from the

Donbas town of Luhansk that was shelled by separatists, Yakimchuk introduces elements of linguistic experimentation partially borrowed from Ukrainian futurists and repurposed to reconstruct the processes of apathetic destruction of language as a result of warfare. The outcome of her experiment is striking; as we can see in her emblematic poem "Decomposition" ("Rozkladannia"), she registers dislocation of the human psyche and speech undone by fear and pain.

And Yakimchuk is not the only author who seeks for a language to render the personal political. Anastasia Afanasieva and Oksana Lutsyshyna are only a few of the innovative voices that form a pleiad of the younger poets who strive to depict how the hybrid war intervenes with private life, and how the very idea of the private, "protected" human existence is shattered and undone by political aggression. In their poems in this volume we find various depictions of the destruction that enters the everyday existence of the Donbas civil population: these poets show how war enters and becomes a part of everyday life (*byt*), where the smell of the rotten fruit (one of the anthology's popular and most disturbing images) of the abandoned crops becomes nauseatingly mixed with the smell of the rotten human flesh.

Pro-Ukrainian Poetry in Russian

Another exciting layer to this poetic multivoicedness is how poetry reflects the political tension of poets who identify themselves with Ukrainian political goals and the building of a national identity, but still write in Russian.[4]

Arguably, the most developed political-cum-aesthetic angle here belongs to Boris Khersonsky, a Ukrainian Russian-language poet of Jewish origin residing in Odesa, who started to write poetry in Ukrainian after the outbreak of war, and whose recent writing has attracted much attention both in Ukraine and Russia. His poetry investigates the languages of Russian imperialist discourses and how they function today. Khersonsky might be the most observant and creative literary reader and critic of the Putin empire's propagandistic language and its highly sophisticated and, alas, effective apparatus. Khersonsky's poems in the anthology, translated by me and Ostap Kin, present a difficult yet exciting problem for a translator. Each of Khersonsky's poems is a showcase, a tapestry of the relics of the Soviet empire (as such it might be compared to Loznitsa's film soundtrack—yet while Loznitsa attempts to recreate the noise and fury of the barricades, Khersonsky records *the noise of time*, the seductive and yet nauseating noise of a nostalgic memory of the Soviet empire—and it is this nostalgic quality that the poet critiques).

In Khersonsky's parodic attention to the workings of the propaganda apparatus is an argument for disturbing connections between the current Russian regime's propaganda methods and those used in the previous wars of the Soviet Empire, especially during the so-called "Great Patriotic War," which during the following decades became the foundation of Russian post-Soviet identity and still functions as such today under Putin's regime.

* * *

In her programmatic poem, Afanasieva asks, openly following the desperate inquiry of Theodor Adorno:

Can there be poetry after:
Yasynuvata, Horlivka, Savur-Mohyla, Novoazovsk
After:
Krasnyi-Luch, Donetsk, Luhansk
After
Sorting bodies in repose from the dying . . .

In a twist of macabre irony, this anthology testifies that if anything is possible after the war—it is poetry. Maybe because it is the medium most reactive to the traumas and changes within the human means of expression, within language. While the other means and modes of literature need time and concentrated effort of attention to pronounce their observation, poetry has the capacity to react urgently and uses the fact of shattered language as its tragic building material.

Notes

1 The poem recited in Sergey Loznitsa's documentary is an adaptation of Taras Shevchenko's poem *Ieretyk* (1845). See Taras Shevchenko, *Zibrannia Tvoriv, Tom 1: Poeziia 1837-1847* (Kyiv: Naukova Dumka, 2003), 290.

2 This idea is inspired by argumentation by Mark Lipovetsky, "The Formal As Political," lecture given as an AATSEEL keynote address, Austin, Texas, January 9, 2016.

3 On poetry about contemporary events in Donbas, see Yuliya Ilchuk, "Hearing the Voice of Donbas: Art and Literature as Forms of Cultural Protest During the War," *Nationalities Papers*, 45.2 (2017): 256-273.

4 The richest reading of the recent poetry about the war in Donbas, can be found in Vasyl Lozynsky, "Poetic Reflection at the Time of War and Peace," *Krytyka*, March 2014. For another important reading, see Yuri Andrukhovych, "An Emergency Bag with Letters," in *Letters from Ukraine* (Krok, 2016), 4-17.

AUTHORS

Anastasia Afanasieva was born in Kharkiv in 1982. She is the author of six books of poetry and the winner of numerous major literary awards and prizes, including the Debut Prize and the Russian Award, two of the top awards in Russian poetry. Her poetry has been translated into English, German, Italian, Ukrainian, and Belarusian. In the US, her poems in translation have appeared in *Cimarron Review*, *Jacket Magazine*, and *Blue Lyra Review*. She is the translator of Ilya Kaminsky's book *Music of the Wind* (Ailuros, 2012). The English language translation of Afanasieva's poem about refugees won First Place in the 2014 Joseph Brodsky/Stephen Spender Prize Competition.

Vasyl Holoborodko was born in Adrianopil, Luhansk oblast, in 1945. In 1965, due to his alleged anti-Soviet views and refusal to cooperate with KGB, Holoborodko was expelled from the university. His work was banned from publication in the Soviet Union for the following twenty years. The indictment also meant that he had severely limited employment opportunities. From the time of his indictment and through the period of Perestroika, Holoborodko had worked as a miner, builder, and farmer.In 1988, with the change in the political climate, Holoborodko published several collections of poetry and was able to resume his university studies. His work has been translated into English, Portuguese, Polish, German, and other languages. Holoborodko is the recipient of several prizes, including the Shevchenko Prize, the top national literary award in Ukraine.

Borys Humenyuk was born in Ostriv, Ternopil oblast, in 1965. He is a poet, writer, and journalist. He has taken an active part in Ukraine's Revolution of Dignity of 2013. Since 2014, he has been involved in the anti-terrorist operation in the Ukrainian Donbas region. He now serves in a self-organized military unit composed mainly of volunteers.

Yuri Izdryk was born in Kalush, Ivano-Frankivsk oblast, in 1962. He is a poet, novelist, and literary critic from Kalush. In 1986, Izdryk was deployed to the site of the Chernobyl disaster to help clean up the radioactive waste. Since 1990, he has worked as the editor in chief of the avant-garde literary journal *Chetver*. A prominent figure in Ukrainian alternative literature and culture, Izdryk is the author of four novels in Ukrainian: *The Island of Krk and Other Stories* (1993), *Wozzeck* (1997), *Double Leon* (2000), and *AM™* (2004). The English translation of *Wozzeck* appeared in 2006.

Aleksandr Kabanov was born in Kherson in 1968. He studied journalism at the Kyiv State University. An author of eleven books of poetry and numerous publications in major Russian literary journals, Kabanov is said to be one of the leading Russian-language poets of his generation. He has been awarded a number of prestigious literary prizes, among them the Russian Prize, International Voloshin Prize, Antologia Prize, and the *Novy Mir* Literary Magazine Award for the best poetry publication of the year. His poems have been translated into German, English, Dutch, Georgian, Ukrainian, Polish, Kazakh, and other languages. Since 2005, Kabanov has been the chief editor of the journal of contemporary culture *SHO* ("WHAT") and coordinator of the International poetry festival Kyiv Laurels.

Kateryna Kalytko was born in Vinnytsia in 1982. She is a writer and translator. She had published six collections of poetry and two collections of short stories. Her poems have appeared in numerous anthologies of Ukrainian literature, and her works have been translated into English, Polish, German, Hebrew, Russian, Armenian, Italian, and Serbian. Kalytko is an acclaimed translator who translates Bosnian, Croatian, and Serbian works into Ukrainian, having translated works by authors such as Adisa Bašić, Nenad Veličković, and Miljenko Jergović. She received the Metaphora award in 2014 for her translation of Jergović's works. She has been the recipient of many literary fellowships, among them the Central European Initiative Fellowship for Writers in Residence in 2015. Kalytko is also the founder of the Intermezzo Short Story Festival, the only festival in Ukraine exclusively dedicated to the genre of the short story.

Lyudmyla Khersonska was born in Tiraspol, Moldova, in 1964. She is the author of two books of poetry, *Vse Svoi*, named one of the ten best poetry books of 2011, and *Tyl'naia-litsevaia* (2015). Her work has received several literary awards, and she has been named laureate and winner of the Voloshin competition. Her poems appear in many journals, including *Novyi Mir*, *Znamia*, *Kreshchatik*, *Interpoezia*, and *Storony Sveta*, and have been translated into Ukrainian, Lithuanian, and German. She gave poetry readings in Moscow, Kyiv, Lviv, Munich, and New York. Khersonska also translates English-language poets into Russian, including Vladimir Nabokov and Seamus Heaney. She has spoken about Russia's war in Ukraine and read her poetry about the war several times on Radio Liberty. Her latest book, *Tyl'naia-litsevaia*, includes poetic reflections on Russian aggression in Ukraine. Khersonska lives in Odesa.

Boris Khersonsky was born in Chernivtsi in 1950. He studied medicine in Ivano-Frankivsk and Odesa. He initially worked as a neurologist, before becoming a psychologist and psychiatrist at the Odesa regional psychiatric hospital. In 1996 Khersonsky took on an appointment at the department of psychology at Odesa National University, before becoming chair of the department of clinical psychology in 1999. In the Soviet times, Khersonsky was part of the Samizdat movement, which disseminated alternative, nonconformist literature through unofficial channels. Following the collapse of the Soviet Union, Khersonsky came out with seventeen collections of poetry and essays in Russian, and most recently, in Ukrainian. Widely regarded as one of Ukraine's most prominent Russian-language poets, Khersonsky was the poet laureate of the Kyiv Laurels Poetry Festival (2008) and the recipient of the Brodsky Stipend (2008), the Jury Special Prize at the Literaris Festival for East European Literature (2010), and the Russian Prize (2011).

Marianna Kiyanovska was born in Zhovkva, Lviv oblast, in 1973. She is a writer, translator, and literary scholar. She is the author of nine books of poetry and one collection of short stories. She had also translated six single-authored volumes of poetry (from Polish and Belarusian). Kiyanovska is a recipient of prestigious awards, including the Kyiv Laurels Literary Festival Prize (2011). In 2014, Forbes Ukraine named her one of the top ten most influential writers working in Ukraine today. She lives in Lviv.

Halyna Kruk was born in Lviv in 1974. She is a poet, writer of fiction and a scholar of Ukrainian medieval literature. She authored four books of poetry and collected some of Ukraine's top awards for young poets. She also writes books for children and young adults. In 2003 Kruk was the recipient of the Gaude Polonia Fellowship from the Polish Ministry of Culture. She teaches literature at the Lviv University.

Oksana Lutsyshyna was born in Uzhhorod in 1974. She is a writer and translator, and lecturer in Ukrainian studies at the University of Texas in Austin, where she teaches Ukrainian language and Eastern European literatures. She holds a PhD in comparative literature from the University of Georgia. Oksana translates alone or in collaboration with Olena Jennings, Kevin Vaughn, and Daniel Belgrad. Her translations of poems and essays by Vasyl Makhno, Marianna Kiyanovska, Bohdana Matiyash and other Ukrainian authors have appeared in *Postroad Magazine*, *The Wolf*, *Ukrainian Literature: A Journal of Translation*, *St. Petersburg Review*, and other venues. Her original work includes two novels, a collection of short stories, and three collections of poetry, all published in Ukraine. Her most recent novel has been long-listed for the Ukrainian BBC award.

Vasyl Makhno was born in Chortkiv, Ternopil oblast, in 1964. He is a poet, essayist, and translator. He is the author of eleven collections of poetry. His most recent collection, *A Paper Bridge*, appeared in 2017. He has also published two book of essays: *The Gertrude Stein Memorial Cultural and Recreation Park* (2006) and *Horn of Plenty* (2011), and two plays: *Coney Island* (2006) and *Bitch/Beach Generation* (2007). Makhno translated Zbigniew Herbert's and Janusz Szuber's poetry from Polish into Ukrainian, and edited an anthology of young Ukrainian poets from the 1990s. His poems and essays have been translated into twenty-five languages. His poems and essays appeared in English in *Absinthe*, *Agni*, *Consequences*, *Post Road*, *Poetry International*, and others. Two poetry collections, *Thread and Other New York Poems* (2009) and *Winter Letters* (2011), were published in English translation. He is the 2013 recipient of Serbia's Povele Morave Prize in Poetry and BBC Book of the Year Award 2015. Makhno lives in New York City.

Marjana Savka was born in Kopychyntsi, Ternopil oblast, in 1973. She published her first poetry collection, *Naked Riverbeds*, at the age of twenty-one. Eight other books, for which she received several awards, have appeared since then, including four poetry collections and three children's books. A former actress and journalist, she edited *We and She*, an anthology of poems by female writers from Lviv, Ukraine, where she lives. She cofounded, with her husband, the *Old Lion Publishing House*. Marjana is the winner of "Torch" award (1998) and the International Vasyl Stus Prize (2003).

Ostap Slyvynsky was born in Lviv in 1978. He is a poet, translator, essayist, and literary critic. He authored four books of poetry. He was awarded the Antonych Literary Prize (1997), the Hubert Burda Prize for young poets from Eastern Europe (2009), and the Kovaliv Fund Prize (2013). Slyvynsky coordinated the International Literary Festival at the Publishers Forum in Lviv in 2006–2007. In 2016, he helped organize a series of readings titled "Literature Against Aggression" during the Forum. Slyvynsky's translations had earned him the Polish Embassy's translation prize (2007) and the Medal for Merit to Polish Culture (2014). In 2015, he collaborated with composer Bohdan Sehin on a media performance, "Preparation," dedicated to the civilian victims of war in the East of Ukraine. Slyvynsky teaches Polish literature and literary theory at Ivan Franko National University.

Lyuba Yakimchuk was born in Pervomaisk, Luhansk oblast, in 1985. She is a Ukrainian poet, screenwriter, and journalist. She is the author of several full-length poetry collections, including *Like FASHION* and *Apricots of Donbas*, and the film script for *The Building of the Word*. Yakimchuk's awards include the International Slavic Poetic Award and the international "Coronation of the Word" literary contest. Her writing has appeared in magazines in Ukraine, Sweden, Germany, Poland, and Israel. She performs in a musical and poetic duet with the Ukrainian double-bass player Mark Tokar; their projects include *Apricots of Donbas* and *Women, Smoke, and Dangerous Things*. Her poetry has been performed by Mariana Sadovska (Cologne) and improvised by vocalist Olesya Zdorovetska (Dublin). Yakimchuk also works as a cultural manager. In 2012, she organized the "Semenko Year" project dedicated to the Ukrainian futurists, and she curated the 2015 literary program Cultural Forum "Donkult" (2015). She was a scholar in the "Gaude Polonia" program of the Ministry of Culture and National Heritage (Poland). In 2015, Kyiv's *New Time* magazine listed Yakimchuk among the one hundred most influential cultural figures in Ukraine.

Serhiy Zhadan was born in Starobilsk, Luhansk oblast, in 1974. He is a Ukrainian poet, fiction writer, essayist, and translator. He has published over two dozen books, including the poetry collections *Psychedelic Stories of Fighting and Other Bullshit* (2000), *Ballads of the War and Reconstruction* (2000), *The History of Culture at the Beginning of* *the Century* (2003), *Lili Marlen* (2009), and *Life of Maria* (2016). His novels and collections of short stories include *Big Mac* (2003), *Anarchy in the UKR* (2005), *Anthem of Democratic Youth* (2006), and *Mesopotamia* (2014). The English translations of Zhadan's work include *Depeche Mode* (Glagoslav Publications, 2013), *Voroshilovgrad* (Deep Vellum Publishing, 2016) and *Life of Maria and Other Poems* (forthcoming with Yale University Press in 2017). Other translations of his work appear in *PEN Atlas*, *Eleven Eleven*, *Mad Hatters Review*, *Absinthe*, *International Poetry Review*, and the anthologies *New European Poets* (2008) and *Best European Fiction* (2010). In 2014, he received the Ukrainian BBC's Book of the Decade Award, and he won the BBC Ukrainian Service Book of the Year Award in 2006 and again in 2010. He is the recipient of the Hubert Burda Prize for Young Poets (Austria, 2006), the Jan Michalski Prize for Literature (Switzerland, 2014), and the Angelus Central European Literature Award (Poland, 2015). Zhadan lives in Kharkiv, Ukraine.

TRANSLATORS

Polina Barskova is a Saint Petersburg–born poet, prose writer, and scholar. She received her PhD from the University of California at Berkeley. She has authored ten collections of poems in Russian; three collections in English translation, *This Lamentable City* (2010), *The Zoo in Winter* (2010), and *Relocations* (2013); and a collection of short stories in Russian, *The Living Pictures* (2014), for which she was awarded the Andrey Bely Prize (2015). She is an editor of the anthology *Written in the Dark: Five Poets in the Siege of Leningrad* (2016) and coeditor of a collection of scholarly articles, in Russian, *The Narratives in Blockade* (2017). She has authored a monograph "Besieged Leningrad: Aesthetic Responses to Urban Disaster" (forthcoming in 2017). Barskova teaches at Hampshire College and lives in Amherst, Massachusetts.

Uilleam Blacker is a lecturer in comparative culture of Eastern Europe at the School of Slavonic and East European Studies, University College London. His research covers the literatures and cultures of Ukraine, Poland, and Russia. His translations of the work of contemporary Ukrainian writers—including Sofia Andrukhovych, Taras Prokhasko, Taras Antypovych, and Lina Kostenko—have appeared on *Words Without Borders*, in the *Dalkey Archive Best European Fiction* series, and in the journal *Ukrainian Literature in Translation*. He is also a member of the UK-based Ukrainian theatre group *Molodyi Teatr London*.

Alex Cigale's own English-language poems have appeared in such journals as the *Colorado Review*, *The Common Online*, and *The Literary Review*, and his translations of Russian Silver Age and contemporary poets in *Harvard Review*, *Kenyon Review*, *Modern Poetry in Translation*, *New England Review*, *PEN America*, *TriQuarterly*, *Two Lines*, *Words Without Borders*, and *World Literature Today*. In 2015, he was awarded an NEA Fellowship in Literary Translation for his work on the St. Petersburg philological school poet Mikhail Eremin, and guest-edited the Spring 2015 Russia Issue of the *Atlanta Review*, writing about it for Best American Poetry. His first full book, *Russian Absurd: Daniil Kharms, Selected Writings* is just out in the Northwestern University Press World Classics series. From 2011 to 2013, he was an assistant professor at the American University of Central Asia, and more recently, a lecturer in Russian literature at CUNY/Queens College.

Boris Dralyuk is a literary translator and the executive editor of the *Los Angeles Review of Books*. He holds a PhD in Slavic languages and literatures from UCLA. His work has appeared in the *Times Literary Supplement*, *The New Yorker*, *London Review of Books*, *The Guardian*, and other publications. He is the translator of several volumes from Russian and Polish, including, most recently, Isaac Babel's *Red Cavalry* (Pushkin Press, 2015) and *Odessa Stories* (Pushkin Press, 2016). He is also the editor of *1917: Stories and Poems from the Russian Revolution* (Pushkin Press, 2016), and coeditor, with Robert Chandler and Irina Mashinski, of *The Penguin Book of Russian Poetry* (Penguin Classics, 2015). His website is bdralyuk.wordpress.com.

Katie Farris is the author of *boysgirls* (Marick, 2011), which combines prose poetry, fairy tale, riddle, myth, and drawings. She has contributed translations to books of Russian, French, and Chinese poetry, including *This Lamentable City* (Tupelo, 2010) and *New Cathay* (Tupelo, 2013). She teaches in the MFA program at San Diego State University and in New England College's low-residency MFA program.

Tatiana Filimonova is a native of Saint Petersburg, Russia. She received a PhD in Slavic languages and literature from Northwestern University and has taught Russian language, literature, and culture at Northwestern, Vanderbilt University, and the College of Wooster. As a scholar of contemporary Russian literature, Tatiana's research lies at the intersection of literature, history, and contemporary politics. She has a special interest in empire studies, Eurasianism, nationalism, regionalism, and postmodernism. Tatiana has published articles on contemporary Russian writers such as Vladimir Sorokin and Pavel Krusanov, as well as on contemporary film.

Sibelan Forrester has translated poetry from Croatian, Russian, and Serbian, including most recently work by Maria Stepanova, Marianna Geide, and Dmitri Prigov. She has made conference presentations on the stories of Marko Vovchok, and is a past president of the Association for Women in Slavic Studies. She teaches Russian language and literature at Swarthmore College.

Amelia M. Glaser is an associate professor of Russian and comparative literature at the University of California San Diego, where she currently directs the Russian, East European, and Eurasian studies program, the Jewish studies program, and *Alchemy*, an online journal of student translation. She is the author of *Jews and Ukrainians in Russia's Literary Borderlands: From the Shtetl Fair to the Petersburg Bookshop* (Northwestern University Press, 2012), the translator of *Proletpen: America's Rebel Yiddish Poets* (University of Wisconsin Press, 2005), and the editor of *Stories of Khmelnytsky: Competing Literary Legacies of the 1648 Ukrainian Cossack Uprising* (Stanford University Press, 2015).

Bob Holman, who wrote the introduction to Serhiy Zhadan's book of selected poems in English ("What We Live For, What We Die For," Yale University Press, 2018) is a poet, professor (currently at Princeton), and founder of the Bowery Poetry Club. He often appears on stage with Yara Arts Group.

Yuliya Ilchuk is an assistant professor of Slavic literatures at Stanford University. She earned her BA in Russian as a foreign language from National Pedagogical University in Kyiv (Ukraine), MA in comparative literature from Kyiv-Mohyla Academy, and PhD in Slavic languages and literatures from the University of Southern California. Her major research interests fall under the broad heading of cultural exchange, interaction, and borrowing between Russia and Ukraine. She has published articles on the topics of postcolonial theory and criticism, institutions of authorship, reading culture, protest art, and post-Soviet identity. Currently, she is working on a book project, titled *Nikolai Gogol: Performing Hybridity*.

Andrew Janco is a digital scholarship librarian at Haverford College. He holds a PhD in history from the University of Chicago. With Olga Livshin, he has translated a number of Russian and Ukrainian poets. His translations are published in *Contemporary Russian Poetry: An Anthology* and several journals.

Olena Jennings's collection of poetry *Songs from an Apartment* was released in January 2017 by Underground Books. Her translations of poetry from Ukrainian can be found in *Chelsea*, *Poetry International* and *Wolf*. She has published fiction in *Joyland*, *Pioneertown*, and *Projectile*.

She completed her MFA in writing at Columbia and her MA focusing in Ukrainian literature at the University of Alberta.

Mary Kalyna is the daughter of post–World War II Ukrainian refugees. A lifelong social justice activist, she organized events in Philadelphia in support of the Maidan. A graduate of Cornell University with an MBA from the Wharton School, she is a writer and researcher whose current focus is documenting the experience of Ukrainian forced laborers in Nazi Germany.

Ilya Kaminsky was born in Odesa, former Soviet Union, in 1977, and arrived in the United States in 1993, when his family was granted asylum by the American government. Ilya is the author of *Dancing in Odessa* (Tupelo Press) which won the Whiting Writer's Award, the American Academy of Arts and Letters' Metcalf Award, the Dorset Prize, and the Ruth Lilly Fellowship given annually by *Poetry Magazine*. *Dancing in Odessa* was also named Best Poetry Book of the Year by *ForeWord Magazine*. Kaminsky was awarded Lannan Foundation's Literary Fellowship. Poems from his new manuscript, *Deaf Republic*, were awarded *Poetry* Magazine's Levinson Prize and the Pushcart Prize. Recently, he was on the short list for Neusdadt International Literature Prize. His anthology of twentieth-century poetry in translation, *Ecco Anthology of International Poetry*, was published by HarperCollins in March 2010. Kaminsky has worked as a law clerk for San Francisco Legal Aid and the National Immigration Law Center, and, more recently, as the Court Appointed Special Advocate for Orphaned Children in Southern California. He is a professor of poetry at San Diego State University.

Maria Khotimsky teaches Russian language and literature and supervises the Russian language program at the Massachusetts Institute of Technology. She has received her PhD from the department of Slavic languages and literatures at Harvard University in 2011. Her research focuses on the history and theory of poetic translation in the Soviet and post-Soviet eras, and on the cross-influences between translation and original writing. She has published several articles devoted to the poetics of translation, and she is a contributor and coeditor of an anthology of scholarly articles devoted to Olga Sedakova's poetry: *Olga Sedakova: Stikhi, Smysly, Prochteniia. Sbornik Nauchnykh Statei* (Moscow: NLO, 2016).

Ostap Kin published work in *The Common*, *Poetry International*, *St. Petersburg Review*, *Springhouse*, *Trafika Europe*, *Ohio Edit*, and in anthologies. He has edited the anthology "New York Elegies: Ukrainian Poetry on the City" (forthcoming with Academic Studies Press). Kin lives in Brooklyn, New York.

Anatoly Kudryavitsky lives in Dublin, Ireland, where he is the editor of *Shamrock Haiku Journal*. He has published four collections of his poetry, the latest being *Horizon* (Red Moon Press, 2016), and three novels (the latest title is *DisUNITY* [Glagoslav, 2013]). His anthology of Russian poetry in English translation, *A Night in the Nabokov Hotel*, appeared in 2006; his anthology of German-language poetry in English translation, *Coloured Handprints*, in 2015; both have been published by Dedalus Press. He edited two anthologies of Irish haiku, *Bamboo Dreams* (Doghouse, 2012) and *Between the Leaves* (Arlen House, 2016). He has also published his English translations from Tomas Tranströmer, Miron Białoszewski, and a few other poets. In 2003, he won the Maria Edgeworth poetry prize. In 2016, one of his poems has been nominated for the Pushcart Prize by *The American Journal of Poetry*. He also was the recipient of multiple international awards for his haiku.

Svetlana Lavochkina is a novelist, poet and translator, born and educated in Ukraine, and currently residing in Leipzig, Germany. In 2013, her novella "Dam Duchess" was chosen runner-up in the Paris Literary Prize launched by Shakespeare & Company and the De Groot Foundation. Her debut novel, a historical burlesque, *Zap*, was shortlisted for Tibor & Jones Pageturner Prize 2015 in London and will be published in the United States in 2017. Svetlana's work has appeared or is forthcoming in numerous literary magazines and anthologies in the United States and UK, including *AGNI*, *New Humanist*, *Poem*, *Eclectica*, *Straylight*, *Circumference*, *Superstition Review*, *Witness*, *Cerise Press*, *Drunken Boat*, *The Literary Review*, *Chamber Four Fiction Anthology*, and elsewhere. Her experimental mono-musical, "Tumbleweed," scored by Patrick Flanagan, was broadcast on Radio Blau in May.

Olga Livshin is an English-language poet, essayist, and literary translator. Born in Odesa and raised in Moscow, she came to the United States as a teenager with her family. Her work has been recognized by the *CALYX* journal's Lois Cranston Memorial Prize, the Poets & Patrons Chicagoland Contest, the Cambridge Sidewalk Poetry Project, and the Robert Fitzgerald Translation Prize (twice). Her poetry and translations are published in

International Poetry Review, *Blue Lyra*, and *Mad Hatters' Review*, among others, and are included in *Contemporary Russian Poetry: An Anthology*, *The Anthology of Chicago*, and *The Persian Anthology of World Poetry* (in Persian translation). Livshin holds a PhD in Slavic languages and literature and has taught Russian at Boston University and Swarthmore College. She lives in the Philadelphia area with her partner Andrew Janco and their little son.

Oksana Lushchevska is a writer and translator. She is an author of children's and young adult books written in Ukrainian. Oksana received her BA in Ukrainian language and literature, English language and literature, and world literature from the Pavlo Tychyna Uman State Pedagogical University. She completed a master's degree in Russian and comparative literature and a graduate certificate in children's literature from the Pennsylvania State University. Oksana studied for a PhD degree in education and taught children's literature courses at the University of Georgia. Oksana is a cofounder of "Kazkarka," now part of *Chytomo* literary website. She is also an initiator of "A Step Ahead: Becoming Global with Ukrainian-English Bilingual Picturebooks" project, aimed at publishing and promoting quality bilingual children's books. Oksana's texts were translated into multiple languages including English, German, and Polish.

Oksana Lutsyshyna is a Ukrainian writer and translator, and lecturer in Ukrainian studies at the University of Texas in Austin, where she teaches Ukrainian language and Eastern European literatures. She holds a PhD in comparative literature from the University of Georgia. Oksana translates alone or in collaboration with Olena Jennings, Kevin Vaughn, or Daniel Belgrad. Her translations of poems and essays by Vasyl Makhno, Marianna Kiyanovska, Bohdana Matiyash, and other Ukrainian authors appeared in *Postroad Magazine*, *The Wolf*, *Ukrainian Literature: A Journal of Translation*, *St. Petersburg Review*, and other venues. Her original work includes two novels, a collection of short stories, and three collections of poetry, all published in Ukraine. Her most recent novel has been long-listed for the Ukrainian BBC award.

Valzhyna Mort is the author of Factory of Tears and Collected Body (Copper Canyon Press 2008 and 2011). She has received the Lannan Foundation Fellowship, the Bess Hokins Prize from Poetry, the Amy Clampitt Fellowship, and the Burda Prize for Eastern European authors. With Ilya Kaminsky and Katie Farris, Mort co-edited Gossip and Metaphysics: Russian Modernist Poems and Prose (Tupelo Press 2014). Born in Minsk, Belarus, she teaches at Cornell University.

Michael M. Naydan is Woskob Family Professor of Ukrainian Studies at The Pennsylvania State University and works primarily in the fields of Ukrainian and Russian literature and literary translation. He has published over forty articles on literary topics and more than seventy translations in journals and anthologies. Of his more than thirty books of published and edited translations, his most recent include Andrei Sinyavsky's *Strolls with Pushkin* (Columbia University Press, 2016) and Igor Klekh's *Adventures in the Slavic Kitchen: A Book of Essays with Recipes* (Glagoslav Publishers, 2016), both co-translated with Slava Yastremski, and Yuri Vynnychuk's *The Fantastic Worlds of Yuri Vynnychuk* (Glagoslav Publishers, 2016). He has received numerous prizes for his translations including the George S.N. Luckyj Award in Ukrainian Literature Translation (2013) from the Canadian Foundation for Ukrainian Studies.

Bohdan Pechenyak was born and raised in Lviv, Ukraine, immigrating to the United States in 1998 and graduating from Arcadia University (BA in sociology) and Temple University (MSW, MPH). He is a firm believer in interdisciplinary approaches, and, in his life, attempts to balance activism, scholarship, and creative pursuits. His interests in the arts include film, writing, and translation.

Wanda Phipps is the author of the books *Field of Wanting: Poems of Desire* (BlazeVOX[books]) and *Wake-Up Calls: 66 Morning Poems* (Soft Skull Press). She received a New York Foundation for the Arts Poetry Fellowship. Her poems have appeared in over one hundred literary magazines and numerous anthologies. She has worked with Virlana Tkacz on translating Ukrainian poetry since 1989.

Anton Tenser was born in Novosibirsk and lived in Kiev until immigrating to the United States in 1989. He holds a PhD in linguistics from the University of Manchester, UK. As a linguist, Anton specializes in the Romani (Gypsy) language; he described the grammar of the Lithuanian Romani dialect, and authored several articles on Romani language and ethnography. His original poems have appeared in *Polutona*, *TextOnly*, and *Vozdukh*; his translations have appeared in *TextOnly*, *Brooklyn Rail*, *InTranslation*, and *Atlanta Review*, among others. He works as a linguist in San Diego and the University of Helsinki but lives in rural Ohio.

Virlana Tkacz is the artistic director of Yara Arts Group, a resident theatre company at La MaMa Experimental Theatre in New York. She has created over thirty shows with poetry she helped translate from Ukraine, Central Asia and Siberia. She received an NEA Poetry Translation Fellowship for her translations with Wanda Phipps of Serhiy Zhadan's poetry. www.brama. com/yara.

Kevin Vaughn is a poet and literary translator who is currently a doctoral student in English and creative writing at the University of Georgia. He also holds an MFA in creative writing from Columbia University. Kevin is a former Fulbright fellow to Jagiellonian University in Poland and a graduate fellow of the Cave Canem Foundation. His poems and translations have appeared in *Callaloo, Crab Orchard Review, Harpur Palate, Mississippi Review, Mythium, Naugutuck River Review, PANK*, and the anthologies: *Killer Lines: Poems about Murder & Mayhem* and *The Southern Poetry Anthology, Volume V: Georgia*. He has been the recipient of artistic residencies all over the world, including The Millay Colony for the Arts, Vermont Studio Center, and Performing Arts Forum in Picardie, France.

Katherine E. Young is the author of *Day of the Border Guards*, 2014 Miller Williams Arkansas Poetry Prize finalist, and two chapbooks. Her poems have appeared in *Prairie Schooner, The Iowa Review, Subtropics*, and others. Young is also the translator of *Two Poems* by Inna Kabysh; her translations of Russian poets Xenia Emelyanova and Inna Kabysh won third prize in the Joseph Brodsky-Stephen Spender competitions in 2014 and 2011, respectively. Young's translations have appeared in *Notre Dame Review, The White Review, Words Without Borders*, and *The Penguin Book of Russian Poetry*, among others; a full-length collection of Inna Kabysh's poems was a finalist for the Cliff Becker Book Prize in Translation. In 2015 Young was named a Hawthornden Fellow (Scotland). She was awarded a 2017 Fellowship in Translation by the National Endowment for the Arts and currently serves as the inaugural Poet Laureate for Arlington, VA. http://katherine-young-poet.com/.

GLOSSARY

AK 47 (also known as **Kalashnikov** or *Kalash*) is 7.62×39 mm assault rifle developed in the Soviet Union by Mikhail Kalashnikov. Known for its simplicity, reliability, and utility value, AK 47 is still used by many armies around the globe.

A **balaclava** is a hat that can be rolled down and used as a mask that covers the whole face, leaving openings only for the eyes and mouth. Balaclavas were first used by the British troops during the Crimean War (1853–56) in order to protect their faces from cold weather. Its name derives from the Crimean city of Balaclava, the site of the 1854 Battle of Balaclava, in which Russian imperial forces clashed with the allied forces of the British, the French, and the Ottoman empires. In the twentieth century, balaclavas became associated with activities that require anonymity: they have been used by terrorists and criminals, but also by protesters and political activists who feared government persecution. Russian activist group and music band *Pussy Riot* used colorful balaclavas in their controversial 2012 anti-Putin performance, leading to the imprisonment of two group members. Balaclavas were also widely used in the Maidan protests of 2013–14, due to the protection they offered against the cold and the police authorities.

BM-21 "Grad" is a truck-mounted 122 mm multiple rocket launcher, developed in the early 1960s in the Soviet Union as a replacement for *Katyusha* multiple rocket launcher, which was one of the most successful mass-produced Soviet weapons of World War II. Although the *Grad* system is not as precise as conventional artillery, it can fire forty rockets in twenty seconds, affecting a large area. *Grad* also has the advantage of being mobile—it requires only ten minutes for reloading and only two minutes for getting it ready to move to a different location. *Grad's* mobility allows the separatists to use it for hit-and-run operations on fortifications and security checkpoints, as well as for targeting civilian property and terrorizing the population. *Grads* are used by both sides in the conflict: the Russian-backed insurgents and the Anti-Terrorist Operation forces. The *Grad* attacks against civilians have been a matter of controversy since neither side is willing to claim responsibility for civilian casualties. Many of the Ukrainian military experts and commentators have argued that the insurgents systematically use *Grads* against the civilian population in order to substantiate their claims that the Ukrainian government is conducting deliberate and systematic "cleansing" of Russian-speaking population in the Donetsk and Luhansk regions. The nickname *Grad* (Град) means *hail* in Ukrainian and in Russian; most of the poets in the anthology use *hail* in this double sense, referring both to the rocket launcher that hits indiscriminately and affects a large area, and to the meteorological event from which it gets its nickname.

A **mortar** is a short-distance ballistic weapon designed to land bombs on nearby areas. Mortars are normally used to target areas with a heavy concentration of enemy troops. The use of mortars in an urban setting often results in "collateral damage," that is, destruction of private property and in civilian casualties. Due to its portability and indiscriminateness, mortars are often used for terrorizing and intimidating the civilian population.

OUN is a volunteer battalion that takes its name from the Organization of Ukrainian Nationalists (OUN), founded in the 1920s and characterized by nationalism with proto-fascist leanings, rendering its controversial history a matter of scholarly debate. The OUN battalion is commanded by Nikolai Kokhanivsky. In July 2014, Borys Humenyuk had been elected second in command. Humenyuk's are the only poems appearing in the anthology written by an acting soldier.

Ruskis is the familiar derogatory term the translator had used to stand for **vatniks**, also **vata** (Russian *vatniki* [ватники], a type of cotton-padded winter coat widely worn by soldiers in World War II, the GULAG inmates, and by an impoverished segment of the Soviet population). *Vatnik* originally appeared in Russian internet (or *runet*) as a visual—a meme. The word *vatnik* is used to refer to an uncritical consumer of state propaganda, who identifies as a Russian patriot. In popular meme representations, vatniks embody the common stereotypes about Russians, such as their tendency to alcoholism, aggressive and militant forms of patriotism, unreflective hatred of everything non-Russian, an inchoate commitment to "spirituality" and "morality," and lack of irony. The term *vatnik* alludes to its bearer's subordinate mentality since the coats were commonly worn by lower-ranked soldiers and prisoners, and had low-cut collars, causing the wearer to stoop in order to keep the back of his neck warm and therefore to adopt a servile-looking posture. The identification of pro-Russian anti-government insurgents in Eastern Ukraine as *vatniks* widened the meaning of the term to include such characteristics as excessive aggressiveness, military adventurism, and an imperialist commitment to the reunification of the former Soviet Republics under the auspices of the Russian Federation.

Ukes is a mildly derogatory Ukrainian diaspora term that one of the translators chose to render a Russian derogatory term **ukropy** (укропы), a word for "dill," a potentially invasive garden herb common in the Ukrainian cooking. When applied to a person, the term acquires multiple negative connotations: of something plant-like, spineless, and difficult to get rid of. Initially, the term was used by separatist insurgents and Putin-sympathizers to refer to the Ukrainian army soldiers and volunteer units. However, it quickly came to stand for Ukrainians in general, and more generally, for those affected by "Euro-propaganda."

Zinc coffins were used in the Soviet Union to transport bodies of fallen soldiers back to their homes. During the Soviet invasion of Afghanistan (also known as Soviet-Afghan war of 1979–89), the Soviet soldiers that fell in action were classified as Cargo (*gruz*) 200, and shipped back in coffins made of zinc (also referenced in Svetlana Alexievich's book *Zinky Boys*). The armies of the former Soviet Republics still use Soviet codes for classifying casualties: *Cargo 200* stands for "irrecoverable losses" (i.e., soldiers killed in action), while *Cargo 300* is a code for the wounded soldiers.

GEOGRAPHICAL LOCATIONS AND PLACES OF SIGNIFICANCE

ATO is an acronym for the Anti-Terrorist Operation initiated by the Ukrainian government in 2014. Its main goals were to regain control of the administrative units captured and held by the separatists, to cut off the Russian-backed separatists from the Russian sources supplying them with weapons and military equipment, and to establish tighter control over the Russian-Ukrainian border. For legal reasons, the Ukrainian government has been using this term rather than calling the fighting in the Donbas area from 2014 onward a war.

Crimea is a peninsula located south of the Ukrainian region of Kherson and west of the Russian region of Kuban. Most of its border is constituted by a shoreline, as it is mostly surrounded by the Black Sea and the Sea of Azov. Administratively, Crimea is an autonomous republic of Ukraine, having gained its current status following a referendum on January 20, 1991. In March 2014, following the takeover of the territory by Russian-backed local separatists and Russian Armed Forces in unmarked uniforms, an unauthorized referendum was held. While the results of the referendum had been deemed illegitimate by the international community, they served as a basis for Russian annexation of the Crimea and the city of Sevastopol as federal subjects of Russia.

Strategic Significance: The Crimean peninsula is of strategic importance to the Russian Federation because of the military bases located there. The city of Sevastopol, located on the coast of the Black Sea, is the principal home of the Russian Black Sea fleet. After the dissolution of the Soviet Union, Russia and Ukraine signed a lease treaty that allowed Russia to keep the Black Sea fleet and its military personnel stationed in Sevastopol. In 2010, Ukraine extended the period of lease until 2042.

Symbolic Significance: Crimea acquired symbolic significance in the Russian national mythology after the Russian Empire annexed the Crimean Khanate, then a vassal state of the Ottoman Empire, at the end of the eighteenth century. The sacrifices involved in acquiring and keeping Crimea play a key role in the Russian sense of entitlement to the peninsula. Peter the Great (period of rule: 1682–1725) launched several unsuccessful campaigns against the Crimean Khanate to gain access to the Black Sea. Catherine the Great (period of rule: 1762–96) had annexed Crimea in 1783, an event that involved two Russo-Turkish wars—first to take it, then to keep it. Catherine's adventurism in the Crimea hadn't been unique, and fit into a larger expansionist plan—Catherine significantly extended the imperial borders, absorbing Crimea, the Northern Caucasus, Right-bank Ukraine, Belarus, Lithuania, and Courland, mainly at the expense of the Ottoman Empire and the Polish–Lithuanian Commonwealth. While not all her plans proved successful—for example, she failed to establish the Byzantine patrimony and secure access to the Mediterranean— Catherine did add some 200,000 square miles (520,000 km^2) to Russian territory. The period of Catherine's rule is often referred to as the Golden Age of the Russian Empire.

The symbolic significance of Crimea as a site of Russian heroism had been cemented when the peninsula became a battlefield in the Crimean War (1853–56) and World War II. In both wars, Sevastopol was besieged and heroically, albeit unsuccessfully, defended. The city acquired a near sacral status as a battlefield that demonstrated Russian resilience and military prowess.

In the late nineteenth and early twentieth century, Crimea served as a beloved vacation destination for the Russian aristocracy and wealthy Russians and Ukrainians. Due to its mild climate and natural beauty, it was also a desirable place to relocate during the Soviet period. Political loyalty would often be rewarded with a Crimean country house (*dacha*) or an all expenses ticket (*putevka*) to a Crimean resort. The forcible deportation of the Crimean Tatars, as well as smaller local ethnic communities including Armenians, Bulgarians, and Greeks in 1944, and the 1945 dissolution of the Crimean Autonomous Soviet Socialist Republic (created in 1921) and Crimea's administrative integration into the Russian SSR, had completed the long process of cultural and political absorption of the peninsula into the Russian administrative and symbolic space. In February 1954, Crimea was transferred from the Russian Soviet Federative Socialist Republic to the Ukrainian SSR. Critics of the transfer allege that it was unconstitutional, and personally motivated by the Ukrainian sympathies of the Soviet leader Nikita Khrushchev. Officially, the transfer was presented as motivated by economic reasons; it was also presented a symbolic gesture marking the 300th anniversary of the "Unification of Russia and Ukraine."

The 2014 annexation led to the popularization of the "Crimea Is Ours" (*Krym Nash*) slogan, which has come to be seen as emblematic of the new wave of Russian nationalism and neo-imperialist sensibilities. The annexation of Crimea had been widely interpreted as the beginning of the New Golden Age of the Russian Empire and the first step towards the reunification of the former Soviet Union under the Russian leadership. In the popular imagination, the imperial and the Soviet histories have merged, yielding a single inchoate narrative about Russian greatness and exceptionality.

Identity Tensions and Political Volatility: The indigenous population of the Crimea are the Crimean Tatars. A large portion of their population had been forcibly relocated under the Stalinist regime in 1944. The relocation was intended as a form of collective punishment for the population's alleged collaboration with the Nazi regime. According to the evidence gathered by volunteers in 1960s, 109,956 (46.2%) of the 238,500 Crimean Tatar deportees died of starvation and disease on their way to the Uzbek, Kazakh, and Mari Soviet Republics. However, in 1991 families of survivors started making their way back to the region and reclaiming what they considered ancestral lands. The resettlement made Crimea one of the most ethnically diverse regions of Ukraine, and one where hostilities between different ethnic groups were most apparent. The Autonomous Republic of Crimea had adopted three official languages for the peninsula: Ukrainian, Russian, and Tatar. The situation for minorities had rapidly deteriorated since the annexation, and a number of anti-Putin Tatar activists have been reported missing.

Debaltseve is a city in the Donetsk region located at a strategic highway and railway junction. In January and February 2015, it was a site of heavy fighting between DPR-LPR separatists and Ukrainian armed forces. Pro-Russian insurgents attacked Debaltseve from three sides, encircling the Ukrainian army stationed there, leading to what many survivors have described as a massacre. During the battle, Debaltseve was heavily shelled by *Grad* rockets and artillery, leading to the demolition of most of the buildings in the city. Together with the Battle of Ilovaysk, the Battle of Debaltseve has been interpreted as a major strategic failure on the part of the Ukrainian armed forces, and a major victory for the allegedly self-organized insurgents.

Dnipro (also known as *Dnepr* and *Dnieper*) is a major European river flowing through Russia, Belarus, and Ukraine.

Symbolic Significance: the Dnipro's symbolic significance as the source of power and vitality stems from its association with the Old Rus and now Ukrainian capital of Kyiv and with the region of Zaporizhia (see Zaporizhian Sich) that both stand on it. As a poetic topos, Dnipro figures prominently in the following key historical and literary texts: *The Primary Chronicle of Kyivan Rus* (*Повѣсть Времаньныхъ Лѣтъ*), covering the historical period from 850 to 1110; *The Tale of Igor's Campaign*, an anonymous epic poem that describes a military campaign (1185) of Igor Svyatoslavich against the Polovtsians; Ukrainian *dumas*, epic songs performed by itinerant bards that were especially widespread during the Hetmanate Era (1649–1782); "The Testament" by Taras Shevchenko (1845), a poem that often gets performed at the official ceremonies and state celebrations.

Historical and Political Significance: the Dnipro flows north to south through the center of Ukraine, dividing it into two historically and culturally distinctive regions, known as the Left-Bank and Right-Bank Ukraine, respectively. While some also view these historical terms as corresponding to the later divisions into Eastern and Western Ukraine, the latter terms only came to be widely used in the twentieth century, with the establishment of the Ukrainian People's Republic as a result of the collapse of the Russian Empire in 1917 and Western Ukrainian People's Republic proclaimed in the former Habsburg Empire in 1918; the two states briefly unified in 1919. After the 1921 Soviet-Polish Treaty of Riga, "Eastern" came to refer to the Soviet-ruled part of Ukraine, and "Western" to parts that remained outside Soviet borders until World War II.

From the fourteenth century onwards, most of the Ukrainian territories were part of the Kingdom of Poland and the Grand Duchy of Lithuania, which united in 1569 to form the Polish-Lithuanian Commonwealth. This period also saw the rise of the Zaporizhian Sich, a semiautonomous polity of the Ukrainian Cossacks, whose history had helped shape Ukrainian national identity discourse in the nineteenth and twentieth century. In 1648, the Cossacks rebelled against Polish rule and established a de facto independent state. Over the course of its existence, the Cossack State was at war with the Polish Crown, the Tsardom of Russia, and the Crimean Khanate. In 1654, a controversial Cossack leader, Bohdan Khmelnytsky, signed a treaty that led to the gradual absorption of Cossack lands into the Tsardom of Russia. In 1667, the Polish-Russian treaty of Andrusovo divided the Ukrainian territory into two parts, with the Dnipro serving as a natural borderline: the Left-Bank Ukraine came under the control of Moscow, and the Right-Bank Ukraine remained part of the Polish-Lithuanian Commonwealth until the partitions of Poland (1772–95). As a result, most of the modern-day Ukraine was brought under Russian control, while several regions were absorbed into the Habsburg Empire.

Donetsk and Luhansk are industrial cities and administrative centers of the Donetsk and Luhansk oblasts (administrative regions). The two cities' populations are 929,063 and 425,848, respectively (as estimated by 2016 report released by the State Statistics Service of Ukraine). Together, the two oblasts form what in the Soviet days came to be known as the **Donbas** region (acronym for the Donets basin, after the river Siverskyi Donets, a tributary of the Don, that flows through it). Since April 2014, the cities of Donetsk and Luhansk and portions of the respective oblasts have been controlled by Russian-backed separatists, who had proclaimed these cities as capitals of the Donetsk and the Luhansk People's Republics (most often referred to by using acronyms of *DPR* and *LPR*, respectively). Although *DPR* and *LPR* are two nominally different republics, they operate as a single military unit and share the political goal of being annexed to the Russian Federation.

Over the course of the preceding decade, Donetsk, home base to Ukraine's wealthiest oligarch Rinat Akhmetov (No. 47 in Forbes' The World's Billionaires), had become a symbol of economic growth and stability in the Donbas region, culminating in the construction of a state-of-the-art Donetsk International airport. Built for the Euro 2012 soccer championship and costing nearly one billion dollars, the airport has been reduced to a pile of rubble as a result of the conflict in the region. The Ukrainian army soldiers and volunteers nicknamed "cyborgs" had held it for 242 days, regularly posting widely watched videos to social networks and YouTube. While the cyborgs' desperate prolonged defense of the airport had been a source of inspiration and pride for many Ukrainians, the destruction of the airport indicates the general sense of chaos, confusion, and devastation in the formerly flourishing region.

The Donbas Humanitarian Crisis: According to a United Nations 2016 report, over 3 million people in Donbas now dwell in the conflict zone: 2.7 million of them live in areas controlled by separatist forces, while 200,000 people reside in the proximity to the contact line. The United Nations Office for the Coordination of Humanitarian Affairs reported in 2016 that 69 percent of households in separatist-controlled areas had difficulty obtaining food due to rising prices and poverty. According to these 2016 figures, the conflict had also created 1.6 million internally displaced persons (IDPs).

Horlivka is a city in the Donetsk region with an estimated population of 256,714. It had been taken over by the separatist forces in April 2014. In July 2014, Ukrainian armed forces attempted to regain control over the city. The unsystematic battles over Horlivka lasted for forty-eight days (July 20–September 6). At the moment, the town of Horlivka remains under separatist control.

Kuban is a region in southern Russia, east of the Azov Sea, with a significant Ukrainian population that for a long time preserved cultural and linguistic ties with Ukraine. In 1932, the Soviets had introduced administrative and educational policies that aimed at obscuring the cultural connections between Kuban and Ukraine. These policies involved replacing the Ukrainian names of sites and places in Kuban with Russian ones and ensuring that all school subjects were taught in Russian. Like Ukraine, Kuban also suffered a heavy hit from the repressions of 1930s and the state-orchestrated famine of 1932–33 known as the Holodomor. While the 1926 Population Census indicates that 49.2 percent of the Kuban population identified as "Ukrainian" (a controversial term that was resisted even by many local Ukrainian-speakers at the time), the 2002 census shows that only 0.9 percent do so.

Mariupol is a city located on the coast of the Sea of Azov, thirty-five miles from the Russian-Ukrainian border, with an estimated population of 461,810. In May 2014, a battle between pro-Russian DPR separatists and the Ukrainian army broke out in Mariupol after it briefly came under DPR control. The city was eventually recaptured by the

Ukrainian state forces, and in June 2014 Mariupol was established as the provisional administrative capital of the Donetsk Region in the place of the separatist-controlled Donetsk.

Novoazovsk is a city located in the Donetsk region, near the Russian-Ukrainian border, with an estimated population of 11,760. The separatist forces took Novoazovsk in August 2014.

Pervomaisk is a city in the Luhansk region with an estimated population of 38,435. Since April 2014, Pervomaisk has been under the control of the Russian-backed separatists demanding an establishment of the Luhansk People's Republic. As the Ukrainian armed forces attempted to regain control over Pervomaisk, Pervomaisk became a focal point of heavy fighting that resulted in the destruction of numerous buildings in residential areas.

Savur Mohyla is a strategic height located three miles from the Russian-Ukrainian border.

Symbolic Significance: Savur Mohyla is referenced in several Ukrainian *dumas*, folk epic poems performed by itinerant bards (*kobzars*), who had usually used a string instrument of lute family (*kobza*) to accompany their singing. In an influential *duma* about Cossack Morozenko, Morozenko is taken to Savur Mohyla—a hill from where he can see "all of his Ukraine"—to be executed. During World War II, Savur-Mohyla became a focal point of intense fighting between the Red Army and the German forces. To honor the Red Army soldiers who had perished at this site, a war memorial had been erected there in 1963. Like most Soviet World War II memorials, it was constituted by an obelisk, a statue of a Red Army soldier raising his weapon, and a number of horizontal panels depicting the heroic feats of different constituents of the Soviet army. In 2014, the obelisk part of the memorial collapsed due to heavy shelling.

Political Significance: In July 2014, the DPR separatists took control of Savur Mohyla from the outnum bered and encircled Ukrainian troops who had defended it for 12 days. Over the course of fighting over the hill, the site changed hands eight times.

Yasynuvata is a town in the Donetsk Region with an estimated population of 35,836. Its location at the railway junction makes it strategically attractive to both sides. Since April 2014, it has been occupied by Russian-backed separatists. In August 2014, Ukrainian armed forces ventured to retake Yasynuvata from the separatists but their attempts proved unsuccessful.

NOTES TO POEMS

ANASTASIA AFANASIEVA

<u>Notes to "she says we don't have the right kind of basement . . .," pp. 2–3</u>
"*mortar*": See *Glossary*.

<u>Notes to "You whose inner void . . .," pp. 4–5</u>

"*You whose inner void*": An allusion to the eternal flame memorials in the former Soviet Union. To honor the Soviet soldiers who died in World War II fighting against Nazi Germany and to remind of human sacrifices that made the victory possible, the Soviet Government introduced a project of building "Victory Squares" featuring an Eternal Flame. The flame burns out of a metallic cauldron that looks similar to a black—or blackened— void, especially once the fire had been extinguished (as it often had been in the post-Soviet times).

"*as in your heyday in the thirties*": The thirties in the Soviet Union had been marked by forced collectivization, the Famine (*Holodomor*) tragedy of 1932–33 that had mainly affected Ukraine and the heavily Ukrainian-populated Russian region of Kuban, and Stalin's deadly "Great Terror"— an extensive and extremely harsh persecution of Soviet citizens, which commonly led to execution or decades in labor camps.

"*when the Earth burned under your feet*": The poet uses an idiomatic expression (Russian: "земля горит под ногами"), which means "to make a run for it," to run so fast one's feet feel like they are on fire. The line may also allude to scorched-earth tactics—when a retreating or an advancing army burns towns and crops in order to deprive the enemies of food and shelter.

"*the Olympic fire*": Symbol of the Olympic Games, originally commemorating the Greek deity Prometheus, whose gift of fire to the mortals enabled them to cultivate the arts and crafts, and thus helped ensure their survival. The Olympic flame is kept alight throughout the games. In the first half of twentieth century, which was marked by the collapse of empires and rise of dictatorships, the event of the Olympic Games acquired a new ideological significance of celebrating the classical proto-military virtues of sportsmanship and brotherly community of idealized able-bodied citizens. In 1936, the Nazi Propaganda Minister Joseph Goebbels introduced the practice of igniting the Olympic torch in Olympia, Greece, and transferring it to the host city (Berlin). The original idea behind the ceremony of torch relay was to establish a tangible connection between the ancient tradition of the Olympic games—described by Adolf Hitler as "a flame that will never die"—and the newly emerged Nazi dictatorship.

Notes to "Can there be poetry after . . . ," p. 17

"*Yasynuvata, Horlivka, Savur-Mohyla, Novoazovsk / Krasnyi-Luch, Donetsk, Luhansk . . .*": The towns listed in this poem became sites of heavy fighting between the Ukrainian army (the Armed Forces of Ukraine) and the separatist insurgents of the self-proclaimed Donetsk and Luhansk People's republics (DPR and LPR). For information about individual towns, see *Places of Significance.*

VASYL HOLOBORODKO

Notes to The Dragon Hillforts, pp. 22–24

"*Dragon Hillforts*": Usually termed *Serpent's Wall*, the "hills" constitute a system of fortifications made of wooden frames that were gradually filled with soil. Because only separate fragments of the wall survived, it is unclear whether the Serpent's Wall constituted a single continuous fortification. The Serpent's Wall has an approximate total length of 1000 km and stretches from Kharkiv region in eastern Ukraine across the Dnipro river to the historic region of Podillya, thus tying together the Right and the Left banks.

"*Pottery historians — archaeologists — study / where they belong / even radiocarbon dating / can't specify their age*": The debate about the Serpent's Wall's age has political implications. Because a wall of this length could only be built by a sizable and organized labor force, and because a need to defend a large territory could only arise in a politically organized community with a government, this opens the door for speculative interpretations: for example, for an idea that the Slavic people (or proto-Ukrainians) had erected a wall to protect their state prior to the Viking establishment of the Kyivan Rus state (862–1240).

BORYS HUMENYUK

Notes to "Our platoon commander is a strange man . . . ," pp. 28–29

"*In the World of Animals*": A Soviet TV program dedicated to zoology and wildlife research.

Notes to "When HAIL rocket launchers are firing . . . ," pp. 33–35

"*Hail*": BM-21 *Grad* multiple rocket launcher. For a more detailed description, see *Glossary*.

"*Mariupol, Artemivsk, Antratsyt*": Cities in Donetsk and Luhansk regions that suffered extensive damage as a result of heavy *Grad* shelling.

Notes to "Not a poem in forty days . . . ," pp. 36–38

"*OUN battalion*": See *Glossary*.

Notes to "An old mulberry tree near Mariupol . . . ," pp. 39–40

"*Mariupol*": See *Places of Significance*.

Notes to A Testament, pp. 42–45

Humenyuk's poem "A Testament" is a response to 1845 poem with the same title written by Taras Shevchenko, the major Ukrainian poet, writer, artist, and political figure. Shevchenko's texts are considered foundational for contemporary Ukrainian literature. Shevchenko was born a serf and was bought out of serfdom by his St. Petersburg artist colleagues. Later in life, he was arrested for anti-imperial political activism as a member of the first modern Ukrainian political organization, the secret Brotherhood of Cyril and Methodius. Shevchenko was imprisoned and sentenced to army service in Central Asia as a private. Due to Shevchenko's harsh criticism of the Russian imperial family in his poem "Dream," Tsar Nicholas I indicated in his sentence that Shevchenko had to remain under close supervision to ensure that he did not have a chance to write or paint. Shevchenko spent over a decade in exile. He died shortly after his return at the age of forty-seven.

"*Donetsk*": See *Places of Significance*.

ALEKSANDR KABANOV

Notes to "This is a post on Facebook, and this, a block post in the East . . . ," p. 52

"*Zinc coffins*": See *Glossary*.

"*the Ukes*" and "*the Ruskis*": See *Glossary*.

"*Merkel*": Angela Merkel is the chancellor of Germany and the leader of Christian Democratic Union (CDU).

"*Kuban battalion*": A fictional battalion; it evokes a revenge fantasy, expressed by some Ukrainian nationalists, of creating a Ukrainian military battalion named *Kuban* that would liberate the region of Kuban from Russian "occupation" and annex it to Ukraine. For the Ukrainian roots of Kuban population, see *Places of Significance*.

"*Couch centurions*": An ironic term referring to a group of Ukrainians with distinct pro-Ukrainian agenda, whose chosen mode of activism was confined to the internet. The term came into usage after the sniper shootings of February 18–21, 2014, which killed about a hundred peaceful protesters in the Maidan Square in Kiev. The murdered protesters had been termed The Heavenly Hundred, the term symbolizing their angelic status as peaceful warriors. At this time, the slogan "Heroes Never Die" also came into popular usage.

Notes to "How I love — out of harm's way . . . ," p. 53

"*Shahid*": An honorary title applied to the faithful who had perished on a religiously sanctioned mission; especially those who had died waging jihad in the military expansion of Islam.

Notes to A Former Dictator, p. 54

"*Balaclava*": See *Glossary*.

"Crimea": See *Places of Significance*.

"*Pale as lard*": The "lard-loving Ukrainian" is a subject of many Soviet-time jokes. Lard does feature prominently in Ukrainian cooking, due to its low cost and relatively low tendency to spoilage.

Notes to "He came first wearing a t-shirt inscribed 'Je suis Christ'. . ." p. 55

"*Je suis Christ*": A reference to the "Je suis Charlie" slogan adopted by supporters of freedom of speech and freedom of the press after the 2015 deadly shooting at the offices of the French satirical newspaper Charlie Hebdo.

"*The golden fish*": An allusion to *The Tale of the Fisherman and the Fish* (Russian: Сказка о рыбаке и рыбке; *Skazka o rybake i rybke*).

"*Transformed . . . into black bread and wine*": An allusion to Jesus's first miracle of turning water into wine, as well as to the doctrine of transubstantiation.

"*Indeed, Pasternak has risen, despite the weak Wi-Fi signal / bringing us a joint for the road, heroin, and some morphine*": A reference to the Russian poet, novelist, and translator Boris Pasternak (1890–1960), awarded the 1958 Nobel Prize for the novel *Doctor Zhivago*. Kabanov's line "bringing us a joint for the road. . ." alludes to a poem "Hamlet" that Pasternak wrote for *Doctor Zhivago* as his character Zhivago's poetry. The word "косяк" used by Pasternak has two meanings: a door jamb (against which the poem's protagonist wearily leans) and a joint (usually filled with marijuana).

Notes to "In the garden of Gethsemane on the Dnieper river . . . ," p. 56

"*Dnieper river*": See *Places of Significance*.

"*Garden of Gethsemane*": A garden at the foot of the Mount of Olives in Jerusalem. According to the biblical account, this was the site where Jesus prayed and his disciples slept the night before Jesus's crucifixion. The Garden of Gethsemane is most closely associated with the kiss of Judas, which led to Jesus's identification and arrest by the police.

"*The two headed cockatoo*": An ironic allusion to the double-headed eagle depicted on the coat of arms of the Russian Federation. The line "parachute turned out to be a balloon" is a related reference the coat of arms of the Russian Airborne troops (Russian: Воздушно-десантные войска России, ВДВ), which features a parachute with a small plane on either side.

Notes to "A Russian tourist is on vacation . . . ," p. 57

"*A Russian Tourist is on vacation*": In the 1990s, the Russian-speaking tourists flooded Egyptian, Turkish, and Asian resorts, generating a stereotype of a heavily-drinking, irate, and entitled "Russian tourist" (popularized also in the ironically patriotic Russian show "Our Russia" ["Nasha Russia"] a knock-off of the British show "Little Britain"). The poet may also be making an ironic reference to the official status of the Russian soldiers who had entered Crimea in 2014 and occupied it. The soldiers were not wearing insignia; when asked what they were doing in the Crimea, they usually responded that they were "just tourists on vacation."

BORIS KHERSONSKY

Notes to "explosions are the new normal, you grow used to them . . . ," p. 88

"*a trigger man and a sapper*": A sapper's task is to plant an explosive device, while a trigger man is responsible for detonating it. Along with other poems from the cycle *My Brother Brought War* (Russian: *Брат Принес Войну*) this poem alludes to the terrorist bombings carried out by pro-Russian separatists in Kherson, Zaporizhzhia, Dnipropetrovsk and Odesa, where Khersonsky resides. One such anonymous terrorist bomb had been planted in front of Khersonsky's apartment.

"stalky Ukrainians — where granny tends to a garden patch": This line, describing Ukrainians growing like plants in granny's garden patch, is a reference to the derogatory term *ukropy* ("dill stalks"). For more detailed information, see *Glossary*.

Notes to "all for the battlefront which doesn't really exist . . ." p. 89

"battlefront which doesn't really exist": A reference to the ambiguous status of the conflict in the Donbas region. The Ministry of Defense of the Russian Federation and Russian President Vladimir Putin deny Russian military intervention in Ukraine despite extensive evidence to the contrary (including aerial images of Russian tanks and artillery pieces concentrated near the demarcation line, trophy military equipment manufactured only in Russia, and the confessions of a number of soldiers with Russian citizenship who had been captured as prisoners of war). The Russian administration insists that Russia's support of LPR and DPR is confined to sending humanitarian aid to Donetsk and Luhansk regions, the insistence that is referenced in Yakimchuk's poem "he says," in which the trucks that allegedly carry humanitarian aid turn out to smuggle artillery.

The poem takes the Russian perspective, encompassing both the latest conflict and the enormous sacrifices that the Russian and Soviet governments had consistently demanded of its people through the use of future-oriented and common-good-emphasizing ideology. This dimension of the Soviet ideological apparatus is poignantly depicted in Svetlana Alexievich's book *Enchanted by Death*.

Notes to "way too long the artillery and the tanks stayed silent in their hangars . . ." p. 91

"Briansk wolf": A term for an ex-convict who had either escaped or was released from a GULAG—a Soviet forced labor camp. Terms

"Briansk wolf" and "Tambov wolf" belong to *blatnoi yazyk*—a cryptolect characteristic of the Soviet *Thieves in Law* phenomenon. The Soviets had the policy of mixing the so-called "Enemies of the People," often members of intelligentsia who were suspected of anti-Soviet sympathies, with proper criminals and bandits, in order to intimidate the former and ensure that their living conditions were intolerable. The term refers to the "criminal proper," and not to those prisoners of the gulags who had been convicted on a political basis. The term "Briansk wolf" was regularly used by the police or regular citizens to refer to ex-convicts; it was also used by the ex-convicts themselves, as a mocking response to "proper Soviet citizens":
— Comrade X . . .
— Let a *Briansk wolf* be your comrade.

Notes to "when wars are over we just collapse . . . ," p. 92

"and where in the world is our victory flag": As of 2016, Russia has an extensive culture of looking back nostalgically to victory in World War II. Victory Day, May 9, is interpreted as the day of Nazi Germany's capitulation to the Soviet Union, and is celebrated ever more lavishly and enthusiastically in Putin's Russia. References to Stalin's role in winning the war predominate. Parades showcase military technology, some of which echoes the technology of the 1940s. As a result, subsequent wars in which Russia is involved are often viewed through the prism of fighting and winning World War II.

"where are the iron sword and the shield of brass": The sword and shield were symbols of the KGB.

Notes to "modern warfare is too large for the streets . . . ," p. 93

"goodbye pretty girls / goodbye company store": The Soviet song implicitly quoted by the poet in these lines focuses on "the Bomb" as a key trope of the Cold War fear-driven discourse. In most Soviet versions, the song represents the perspective of American soldiers on a mission to destroy the Soviet Union. The song appropriates a famous American coalminer's song "Sixteen Tons" first recorded in the forties in Kentucky.

"*Kalashnikov*": see *Glossary*

"*firemen and militia are looking for him, he's the real hero*": A reference to the poem "The Tale of a Hero that Nobody Knows" by the Soviet children's poet Samuil Marshak. In Marshak's poem, the police and the firemen are looking for an unidentified twenty-year-old who had performed a heroic act of rescuing a girl from a burning building. In Khersonsky's poem, the ordinary-looking guy is not sought out as a hero, but wanted on suspicion of criminal terrorist activity.

OKSANA LUTSYSHYNA

Notes to "eastern europe is a pit of death and decaying plums . . . ", pp. 116–117

"*Miklós Radnóti*": Birth name Miklós Glatter (1909–44), a Hungarian Jewish poet who had perished in the Holocaust. Radnóti had been conscripted by the Hungarian Army; as a Jew, he was assigned to an unarmed "labor battalion." In August 1944, as Yugoslav anti-Nazi partisans led by Josip Tito advanced, Radnóti's group of 3,200 Hungarian Jews was force-marched to central Hungary, with most of them—including the poet—perishing along the way. Witnesses reported that Radnóti was severely beaten by a drunken militiaman who had been harassing him for his "scribbling." Due to fact that the local hospitals had been demolished by carpet bombing, prisoners who required medical assistance were executed. Radnóti was shot along with some other Jews and buried in a mass grave. His last poem was dedicated to his friend Miklós Lorsi, who was shot to death during their death march.

VASYL MAKHNO

Notes to February Elegy, p. 122

"*Shevchenko*": Taras Hryhorovych Shevchenko, see note to Borys Humenyuk's "Testament."

Notes to War Generation, p. 123

"Dnipro (Dnieper)": See *Places of Significance*.

Notes to On Apollinaire, p. 125

"Apollinaire": French poet Guillaume Apollinaire (1880–1918) fought in World War I. In 1916, he received a shrapnel wound to the temple. While recovering from the wound, he coined the term "Surrealism." Shortly after, Apollinaire died of influenza during the Spanish Flu pandemic of 1918. While at the front and during his recovery, Apollinaire wrote highly influential modernist poems describing his war experiences, often using the technique of automatic writing. For a striking example that adopts a delirious intoxicated-like perspective on the events, rendering them as aesthetic experiences, see "Wonder of the War."

LYUBA YAKIMCHUK

Notes to Decomposition, pp. 152–153

"Pervomaisk": See *Places of Significance*.

"Debaltsevo": Also Debaltseve; see *Places of Significance*.

Notes to Crow, Wheels, p. 158–159

"BTR": Also known as a "light tank" is a Russian-made amphibious armored vehicle equipped with a machine gun and a small- to medium-caliber main gun. *BTR*'s primary function is to transport infantry to the battlefield.

SERHIY ZHADAN

Notes to Sect, pp. 169–170

"Sect": The Evangelical Protestant presence in Ukraine dates back to the nineteenth century. Despite having been prohibited in Soviet Ukraine since

1920s, these communities persisted through the Soviet days. In the 1990s, after the disintegration of the Soviet Union, the Evangelical Protestant and Baptist communities experienced a revival, increasing rates of conversion and rising to greater visibility. The religious vacuum generated by the Soviet anti-religion policies, and the humanitarian assistance such as food and clothing that was regularly distributed through these communities contributed to their growth. The Protestants in Ukraine now account for 2 percent of Ukraine's population. Nevertheless, these groups are still commonly regarded with suspicion and referred to as "sects," an attitude encouraged by traditional Greek Catholic and Orthodox churches of Ukraine.

ACKNOWLEDGMENTS

We are deeply grateful to all contributors for their excellent work and for their patience with us. The anthology couldn't have happened without the goodwill of the authors, who had entrusted their work to us; and the translators, all of whom were willing to take up the project as a labor of love.

Special thanks go to the wonderful and supportive team of the Academic Studies Press. We are thankful to the Ukrainian Series Editor Vitaly Chernetsky, who had endorsed the project and trusted us to take it on. His thoughtful comments and suggestions helped the project take the shape it did, and challenged us to keep improving it to the very end. We couldn't have completed the anthology without the generous support and expertly advice of ASP's acquisitions editors, Meghan Vicks, Faith Stein, and Oleh Kotsyuba. Meghan helped the project take off, both conceptually and financially, facilitating the applications for NEH and HURI funding. Faith saw that project take more definitive shape, offering sensitive guidance at every step. Oleh's thoughtful suggestions helped us improve the project at its final stages and bring it to completion. His enthusiasm, grace, and support have inspired us to keep going when we most felt like giving up.

The project had also benefited from the support of friends, colleagues, and mentors. Andriy Zayarnyuk reviewed the scholarly apparatus with an eye to historical plausibility and helped us refine and improve it. Kevin Vaughn spent countless hours on Skype editing the translations with us to the din of the streets of Paris, Berlin, and Prague, and the birdsongs of Lviv and Arkansas. Working with him was both inspiring and humbling. Discussions with Olena Haleta had helped us refine our conception of the project at its earliest most vulnerable stages. Oksana Lutsyshyna gave her unending support in bridging gaps and building bridges and continually helped us communicate with authors and translators. Polina Barskova's rigorous questioning led us out of the woods when we found ourselves stalling. Ilya Kaminsky suggested that the anthology spill over into an on-going virtual project, encouraging us to keep working on new translations and adding new names.

234

We are also thankful to venues that had published works that appear in this anthology, drawing greater attention to our authors and translators.

Oksana Maksymchuk and Max Rosochinsky

ACKNOWLEDGMENT OF PRIOR PUBLICATION

Anastasia Afanasieva, From "Cold" and "The Plain Sense of Things," translated by Ilya Kaminsky and Katie Farris, *Blue Lyra Review*, issue 1.2, fall 2012, http://bluelyrareview.com/anastasia-afanasieva.

Anastasia Afanasieva, "She says we don't have the right kind of basement in our building," translated by Oksana Maksymchuk and Max Rosochinsky, *The London Magazine*, April–May, 2015.

Anastasia Afanasieva, "She Speaks," translated by Olga Livshin and Andrew Janco, *Blue Lyra Review*, Issue 5.3, Fall 2016.

Borys Humenyuk, "Our platoon commander is a weird fellow," "When you clean your weapon," translated by Oksana Maksymchuk and Max Rosochinsky, *Cordite Poetry Review*, May 2017, https://cordite.org.au/translations/maksymchuk-rosochinsky-humenyuk/2.

Boris Khersonsky, "Up the ladder with you now, hands tied behind your back," translated by Alex Cigale, *Springhouse Journal*, May 10th, 2016.

Aleksandr Kabanov, "He came first wearing a t-shirt inscribed 'Je suis Christ,'" translated by Alex Cigale, *Poetry International Online*, November 2016, https://pionline.wordpress.com/2016/11/15/five-poems-by-aleksandr-kabanov.

Lyudmyla Khersonska, "Did you know that if you hide under a blanket and pull it over your head," "Buried in a human neck, a bullet looks like a eye, sewn in," "Leave me alone, I'm crying. I'm crying, let me be," translated by Olga Livshin and Andrew Janco, *Adirondack Review*, winter 2016, http://www.theadirondackreview.com/lyudmilakhersonska.html.

Lyudmyla Khersonska, "The whole soldier doesn't suffer," translated by Katherine E. Young, *Words Without Borders*, April 2016, https://www.wordswithoutborders.org/article/april-2016-women-write-war-the-whole-soldier-lyudmyla-khersonska-katherine.

Lyudmyla Khersonska, "The enemy never ends," translated by Katherine E. Young, *Hayden's Ferry Review*, Fall/Winter 2016.

Lyudmyla Khersonska, "I planted a camellia in the yard," "One night, a humanitarian convoy arrived in her dream," translated by Katherine E. Young, *Tupelo Quarterly* 12, June 2017, http://www.tupeloquarterly.com/tag/lyudmyla-khersonska.

Lyudmyla Khersonska, "How to describe a human other than he's alone," "When a country of – overall – nice people," "A country in the shape of a puddle, on the map," translated by Valzhyna Mort, *Poetry International Online*, December 2016, https://pionline.wordpress.com/2016/12/15/four-poems-by-ludmila-khersonsky-translated-by-valzhyna-mort.

Boris Khersonsky, "Bessarabia, Galicia, 1913-1939: Pronouncements," translated by Valzhyna Mort, *Poetry International Online*, December 2016, https://pionline.wordpress.com/2016/12/13/bessarabia-alicia-1913-1939-pronouncements-by-boris-khersonsky-translated-by-valzhyna-mort.

Lyuba Yakimchuk, "Decomposition," "Caterpillar," "How I Killed," translated by Oksana Maksymchuk and Max Rosochinsky, *Letters from Ukraine: An Anthology*, Krok Books, 2016.

Lyuba Yakimchuk, "Crow, Wheels," translated by Oksana Maksymchuk and Max Rosochinsky, *Words Without Borders*, April 2016, http://www.wordswithoutborders.org/article/bilingual/april-2016-women-write-war-crow-wheels-lyuba-yakimchuk-oksana-maksymchuk.

Lyuba Yakimchuk, "Eyebrows," translated by Svetlana Lavochkina, *New Humanist*, Autumn 2016.

Serhiy Zhadan, "Thirty-Two Days Without Alcohol," translated by Ostap Kin, *The Common*, Issue 12, November 2016, http://www.thecommon-online.org/thirty-two-days-without-alcohol.

Serhiy Zhadan, "Take Only What Is Most Important," translated by Virlana Tkacz and Wanda Phipps, *Consequence Magazine*, vol. 8, Spring 2016.

Serhiy Zhadan, "We speak of the cities we lived in," "Now we remember: janitors and the night-sellers of bread," translated by Valzhyna Mort, *Virginia Quarterly Review*, Fall 2011, http://www.vqronline.org/vqr-symposium/stones-excerpts.

INDEX

Printed in the USA
CPSIA information can be obtained
at www.ICGtesting.com
JSHW011946151123
52156JS00012B/423

9 781618 118615